JUNIOR

Date Due

FEB 15 '99			
AUG 16 '00			
JUL 6-20-01			

9 / 98

IN THE LAND OF
THE TAJ MAHAL

IN THE LAND

OF THE

TAJ MAHAL

The World of the

Fabulous Mughals

ED ROTHFARB

Henry Holt and Company
New York

Henry Holt and Company, Inc.
Publishers since 1866
115 West 18th Street
New York, New York 10011

Henry Holt is a registered
trademark of Henry Holt and Company, Inc.

Published in Canada by Fitzhenry & Whiteside Ltd.,
195 Allstate Parkway, Markham, Ontario L3R 4T8.

Library of Congress Cataloging-in-Publication Data
Rothfarb, Ed.
In the land of the Taj Mahal: the world of the fabled Mughals /
by Ed Rothfarb.
p.   cm.
Summary: Describes the history and accomplishments of the Mughal
dynasty, with an emphasis on the period from Babur to Shah Jahan.
1. Mogul Empire—Juvenile literature. [1. Mogul Empire.]   I. Title.
DS461.R64   1997   954.02'5—dc21   97-8281
CIP

ISBN 0-8050-5299-2

First Edition—1998

Book design by Debbie Glasserman

Printed in the United States of America
on acid-free paper. ∞

1 3 5 7 9 10 8 6 4 2

For my parents

— E. R.

Acknowledgments

Writing a book like this required a lot of help, and I am very grateful to the many scholars, curators, and museum personnel who generously helped me. Foremost among them is Catherine B. Asher, of the University of Minnesota, who from the start aided me greatly with access to information and visual materials. She also reviewed the manuscript and meticulously pointed out many errors, helping to make this a better book. In acknowledging the help of experts, I must also say that all errors and opinions expressed in these pages are completely my own.

I also want to thank John Seyller of the University of Vermont; Wheeler M. Thackston, Jr., of Harvard University; Dr. Latifa Hagigi of UCLA; Ellen Smart of the San Diego Museum; Marie Lukens Swietochowski of the Metropolitan Museum of Art, New York; Dr. Milo C. Beach and Simona Cristanetti of the Freer Gallery and Arthur M. Sackler Gallery, Washington, D.C.; Dr. Stephen Markel and Recinda Jeanine of the Los Angeles County Museum of Art; and Dr. Barbara Schmitz of the Morgan Library, New York. In addition, Seema Shahi and Mr. Sharma from the Government of

India Tourist Office, New York, were very helpful, as was Christina Gascoigne, of London.

Thanks are due to the Indo-US Subcommission on Education and Culture for their grant in 1993, which enabled me to get to know India and see its Mughal heritage firsthand. They are also due to my editor, Marc Aronson, for his sage guidance, abiding patience, and generous encouragement.

I want to thank Matt Rosen at Henry Holt, Inc., whose help and enthusiasm brought this book along. Thanks, as well, to Martha Rago and Debbie Glasserman, whose beautiful design evokes the Mughal world in these pages.

Finally, mention must be made of the friends who kindly helped me throughout the process of writing this book; they cooked me dinner, gave encouragement, and heard more about the Mughal dynasty than they bargained for. Many thanks to Marina Budhos, Laurel Berger, Lori Novak, David Sipress and Ginny Shubert, Bob Stortz, and, most of all, with deepest thanks, to Peter Trias.

Contents

x

4. NASIR UD-DIN MUHAMMAD HUMAYUN   69

5. ABU'L FATH JALAL UD-DIN MUHAMMAD AKBAR   91

IN THE LAND OF
THE TAJ MAHAL

Chapter 1

THE BUILDERS

The Emperor's Dream

The Taj Mahal, wonder of the world, place of legends in far off India. Raised by a fabulously wealthy emperor as a tomb for the one he cherished, his beautiful departed wife.

You can journey there. You can walk in its gardens and peer through its gateway. In the early morning, you will see a shimmering image of domes, arches, and towers, gently lit by the rising sun. It will be quiet there, and peaceful. Women, draped in *saris*, light flowing silks of brilliant colors, will glide past to ascend the white marble stairs. In respect, you will leave aside your shoes, as visitors have for centuries. Inside the cool and lofty space you will see the lovers' tombs, lying side by side. From love and sorrow this place was conceived. For remembrance and for beauty it was finally built.

Can anyone explain its mysterious beauty? Its power to draw pilgrims from around the world? It is almost as if the Taj Mahal were not made by ordinary mortals, and, in a sense, it was not. It was created by a splendid dynasty so in love with beauty that its members alone could bring this exquisite dream to life. They were called the Mughals.

THE TAJ MAHAL BY MOON-LIGHT, *ca. 1815, by Sita Ram. Harvard University Art Museums, Cambridge, Arthur M. Sackler Museum.*
The nineteenth-century Indian artist Sita Ram painted two views of the Taj Mahal, one during the daytime, and one on a moonlit night when the monument was at its most magical.

The Mughals ruled over a large part of India for more than three hundred years. They established their dynasty at the same time that Cortés conquered Mexico, but unlike Cortés they did not destroy a civilization. At that time northern India was known as Hindustan, and in that land they built a fabulous empire. While some had invaded only to plunder, they remained to create a heritage of splendor. There were mighty warriors and grandiose kings, fantasy palaces and golden towers, sparkling jewels and gossamer silk—a fabled world long gone, but hardly forgotten.

The Mughals came in the fifteenth century and followed a Central Asian prince named Babur. In their quest for riches, they rode through rugged mountain passes to descend onto Hindustan's plains. The land before them was vast and ancient. It had given the world great religions, rare spices, and precious silks, but invaders were drawn above all by its great wealth. Hindustan was famed for its gems and precious metals. Even its temples, its houses of worship, were said to contain storehouses piled high with treasure. Legends spoke of golden statues studded with rubies, sumptuous necklaces dripping with pearls, diamond crowns, silver shields, and massive golden bowls.

Despite its abundance of riches, Hindustan was not well-defended, and Babur soon conquered. He could have looted the land and left, like his famed ancestor Amir Timur 127 years before. Babur chose a different path. He stayed and founded a dynasty. Within fifty years his heirs forged a brilliant new culture. They enriched the conquered land and gave it order. They built dazzling new cities like Agra and Shahjahanabad, and planned ambitious roads for trade and war.

Some seventeenth-century European travelers who visited the Mughal Empire wrote of a great north-south highway hundreds of miles long, lined for much of its length by four rows of shade trees. It connected the three Mughal capital cities of Agra, Delhi, and Lahore. The path had always been there, and it had been improved and enhanced by Sher Shah, a non-Mughal ruler who reigned from

1540 to 1545. It was maintained by the succeeding Mughal emperors, who constructed serais, or inns, along the route to serve its many travelers. So famous was the road that some contemporary European maps of Hindustan depicted it.

In addition to public works, the Mughals promoted agriculture and made economic reforms. At their dynasty's height, they fostered religious tolerance and revoked age-old discriminatory legislation. In the arts they founded a brilliant new style of painting and left the land with masterworks of beauty, such as the Taj Mahal.

MAP OF INDIA, *designed by William Baffin, engraved by Renold Elstrack, from* Purchas His Pilgrimes *(London, 1625). Chapin Library, Williams College, Williamstown, Massachusetts.* This English map was designed during the reign of Jahangir in the early 1600s, and depicts the great tree-lined highway linking the three imperial capitals of Agra in the south and Delhi and Lahore in the north.

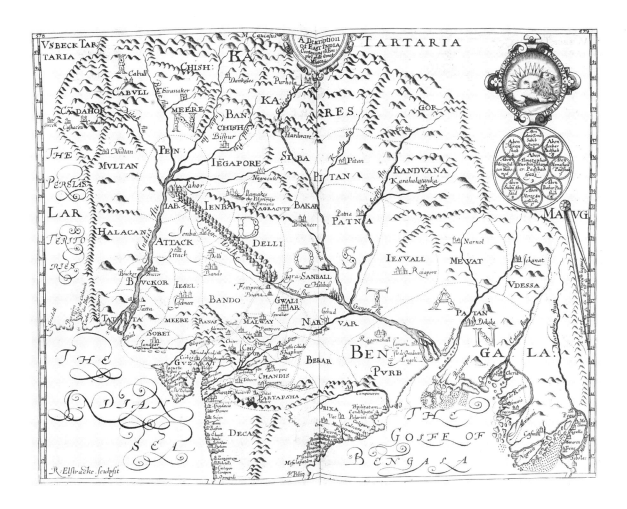

Their emperor was known far and wide as the Great Mughal. His splendor was legendary, like the Peacock Throne from which he ruled. His court drew the great princes and nobles of the land, and within his palace lived the exquisite ladies of the imperial harem. The emperor's treasure was endless, his domains bountiful, and his power absolute.

At the very zenith of its glory the Mughal imperial court was described by François Bernier, a physician from France who visited the empire between 1658 and 1664. He painted an opulent picture of the *durbar,* the ceremony of audience, which, beginning with Shah Jahan, the Great Mughal performed daily for his assembled court.

According to Bernier the emperor's elevated marble throne stood in a magnificent hall whose pillars and ceiling were covered over with beaten gold. Long silver railings enclosed the section for the very highest nobles of the land. Further away stood the lesser nobles, and further yet, filling the immense courtyard beyond, were thousands of the emperor's subjects. With heads bowed and arms crossed they all stood humbly in silent veneration of their lord, the Great Mughal.

During the two-hour ceremony, the imperial elephants, regal beasts adorned with fine cloths, silver ornaments, and tinkling bells, were marched by in a solemn procession. Bernier described it:

> As if proud of his gorgeous attire and of the magnificence that surrounds him, every elephant moves with a solemn and dignified step; and when in front of the throne, the driver, who is seated on his shoulder, pricks him with a pointed iron, animates and speaks to him, until the animal bends on one knee, lifts his trunk on high and roars aloud, which the people consider as the elephant's mode of performing the *taslim,* or usual reverence.

The Mughal Empire waxed strong and glorious but ultimately slid into decline. By the nineteenth century, it had become a shadow of its former self. Finally it collapsed. What remained were its words, its art, and its magnificent structures, silent witnesses to the vanished imperial past.

The Faith of the Mughals

Centuries before the Mughals arrived in India, their ancestors were nomadic warriors living on Central Asia's vast grasslands. Early in their history, they embraced Islam, one of the world's great faiths. In accepting Islam they entered a new world of religious ideals, scholarship, and culture that stretched all across Asia. By the time the Mughals conquered India, they had long been adherents of this faith. Out of their devotion to Islam, they built many beautiful *mosques*, or houses of worship, throughout Hindustan.

The greatest mosque in all of India, the Jami Masjid of Delhi, was built by the Mughal emperor Shah Jahan, who created the Taj Mahal. Its magnificent domes and tall, slender towers still dominate the skyline of the old city. From its opening in 1658 to the middle of the nineteenth century, when it was closed for a time, and up until today, it has been used by Delhi's faithful. Every Friday, the holy day of Islam, thousands fill its courtyard to offer up their prayers in unison, bowing and prostrating themselves as one devout mass.

Islam, their creed, was founded in the sixth century C.E., making it younger than Judaism, Christianity, and Hinduism. But with the energetic fervor of youth, it quickly swept across the world. Today it is estimated that one seventh of the world's population are Muslims, followers of the Islamic faith. One of the largest Muslim populations in the world, more than 100 million, reside in India, the land of the Mughals.

Islam means submission to the will of God, and a Muslim is one who submits to that will. The God of the Muslims is called Allah and, like the God of the Old Testament, he is the one god. Islam, therefore, is a monotheistic faith. Allah, their ever-present God, is just, almighty, and merciful.

Muhammad, whose name means "highly praised," was the great prophet of Islam. According to tradition he was born in Mecca, Arabia, in 570 C.E. In his time Mecca was a great trading center and contained many shrines, none more sacred, though, than the Kaaba. This rectangular structure contained many idols and a large, black meteorite that had fallen from the heavens in the distant past. The local Arab tribes worshiped these idols and the gods that they represented.

In Mecca, Muhammad came into contact with Jewish and Christian merchants and was intrigued by their concept of one god. This contact, and his own questing nature, led him to seek spiritual retreat in the desert. There he would spend periods fasting and meditating. During one such period, he had a divine revelation, a vision of the angel Gabriel, who cried out to him, "Recite!" Falling into a trance-like state, he spontaneously began to recite the first verses of the sacred Quran, the holy book of the Muslims.

This was just the first of his revelations. He had many more, and by the end the entire Quran had been revealed in sublime, poetic Arabic. To Muslims it is the direct word of God, spoken through the Prophet. Muhammad began attracting many followers, and after numerous struggles, including the *Hijra*, his flight from Mecca, he returned there in triumph. Destroying its idols, he reconsecrated the Kaaba to Islam. Since that day Mecca has been a center for pilgrimage for Muslims from around the world.

The new faith spread with the advancing troops of Muhammad's followers. After the great Prophet's death in 632 C.E., it was led by three caliphs, or "successors," Abu Bakr, Omar, and Othman. Under them, all of the Middle East, including the mighty Persian Empire, fell under the banner of Islam. Within one hundred years, the faith spread as far west as Spain and all the way to the borders of Hindustan.

As the Muslim population spread from country to country, they were unified by their common observance of the Five Pillars of

Islam. These were observances prescribed by Muhammad for all of his followers. Islam, unlike Catholicism, has no organized priesthood or sacraments to organize its believers. Rather, the Five Pillars and the sacred Quran bind the community of Muslim faithful around the world.

The Five Pillars are the Muslim acts of faith. The first and foremost is faith in Allah. This is the simplest act and yet the deepest as well. The Muslim confession of faith, the *shahadah* states "There Is No God But Allah, and Muhammad Is His Prophet."

In the reign of the Mughal emperor Akbar (1556–1605), an interesting problem arose concerning the use of Allah's sacred name. The expression "Allahu Akbar" means "God is great." "Akbar," also the emperor's name, means "great." "Allahu Akbar" has been a cry of Muslims since the beginning of the faith. It has been shouted for joy and cried from sorrow, because it acknowledges the supremacy of Allah in all things.

Around the year 1575, the emperor decided that he would like the statement "Allahu Akbar" engraved on his imperial seal and coins. "Allahu Akbar" can either have the proper meaning of "God is Great," or the heretical meaning of "Akbar is God." The emperor denied that any such impudence would ever enter his mind.

The second Pillar of Faith is prayer five times a day, called *Salat* in Arabic. Around the world Muslims face the holy city of Mecca when they pray. From Hindustan one faces west. The call to prayer is announced by the *muezzin*, who chants it from the tall *minaret,* the tower attached to the mosque. Except on the holy day of Friday, it is not necessary to go to a mosque to pray. Since prayer occurs at five regular times throughout the day, a devout Muslim prays wherever he or she happens to be at that time.

Throughout the Muslim world there is a tradition of spreading beautiful prayer carpets on the ground when one prays. Prayer is said while standing. The palms of the hands are opened to the sky, and at moments during prayer, one bows to the carpet and reverently touches it with one's forehead.

IMAGE OF THE KAABA, *poster.*
Collection of Ed Rothfarb.
This popular poster depicts
the holiest site in the Muslim
world, the Kaaba in Mecca.
One of the essential rituals for
all of the faithful who have
undertaken the Hadj, or pilgrimage to Mecca, is circling
this shrine.

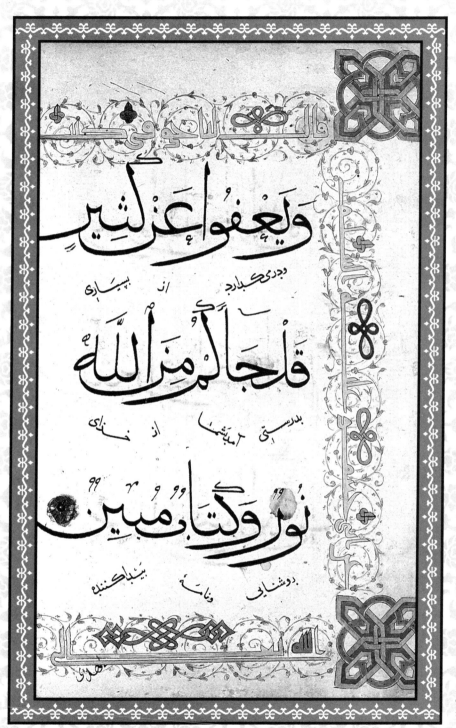

FOLIO FROM THE QURAN, *ca. 1400, provenance unknown; ink, opaque watercolor, and gold on paper, 11⅛ × 7¼". Christian Humann Asian Art Fund, Los Angeles County Museum of Art.* Muslims consider the Holy Quran to be the word of Allah as given to Prophet Muhammad. It is written in Arabic and occupies as central a place in the Muslim religion as the Torah of the Jews, or the New Testament for Christians. Qurans are often beautifully made and have elaborate calligraphy, but they are never illustrated. Depictions of people are forbidden in the orthodox Muslim faith, especially in its most sacred book.

The Mughal emperor Aurangzeb, who reigned from 1658 to 1707, was the most devoutly orthodox ruler of the Mughal world. He was an accomplished military leader as well. In one famous incident, he dismounted in the thick of battle because it was the time for prayer. Surrounded by clashing swords and charging battle elephants, and in full view of his awestruck opponents, he calmly recited his prayers, bowing toward Mecca.

The Third Pillar is giving alms to the poor, or *Zakat*. All Muslims must support both the needy and the community's religious institutions. The Quran states that one should annually give two and one-half percent of one's holdings to the poor. Giving charity, a link between believers, is a key element of the Islamic faith.

The Mughal empress Nur Jahan was the wife of Emperor Jahangir, who reigned from 1605 to 1627. Immensely powerful and wealthy, she was famous for her charities. One of the court chronicles of Jahangir's reign, the *Iqbalnama,* says of her:

> Whoever threw himself upon her protection was preserved from tyranny and oppression; and if she ever learnt that any orphan girl was destitute and friendless, she would bring about her marriage, and give her a wedding portion. It is probable that during her reign no less than 500 orphan girls were thus married and portioned.

The Fourth Pillar is the annual Fast of Ramzan (Ramadan), called the *Suam* in Arabic. The ninth month of the Muslim year, Ramadan, commemorates Muhammad's period of meditation and revelation. It is a time of contemplation and austerity for all Muslims. During Ramadan one must do without all food and drink from sunrise until sunset.

Since the Muslims have a lunar calendar, the month of Ramadan falls at a different time each year. When it falls during summer, long, hot, daylight hours are particularly difficult for the faithful. At night, however, there is feasting, and at Ramadan's end a great holiday like Christmas occurs, with gift-giving and joyful celebration.

The Mughal historian Abd ud-Karim Badauni, who served at Emperor Akbar's court, related a dramatic Ramadan incident from his own life. While traveling with the party of the Muslim nobleman Husayn Khan, his group was attacked by bandits. The attackers were led by a renegade Hindu prince who had been terrorizing the area. A fierce battle ensued with many killed on both sides. Finally, although utterly exhausted, starved, and parched due to the fast, the forces of Husayn Khan prevailed. Badauni relates the experience, in which he was surrounded by dying comrades.

> Some of our men had strength of mind and body enough . . . of maintaining a strict fast. I, on the contrary, in my weakness, at last took a cup of water to moisten my throat, for want of which some poor fellows died.

The laws of Islam consistently advocate moderation and humanely allow the faithful to forgo the fast if they are physically incapable of keeping it. This story from Mughal times shows the extreme devotion that some felt toward keeping the fast.

The Fifth Pillar is the pilgrimage to Mecca, called the *Hadj*. All Muslims are urged to make the journey to the holy city of Mecca at least once in their lives. There they visit the sites of the Prophet Muhammad's life and pay hommage to the Kaaba, the great rectangular structure that still stands at the heart of the city. This pilgrimage is an act that affirms the unity of all believers. Garbed in white garments, they worship together despite their distinct national, racial, or economic backgrounds.

Although no Mughal emperors ever made the pilgrimage to Mecca, many of their relations did. Haji Begum was the senior wife of the Emperor Humayun, who ruled from 1530 to 1556. Her very title, Haji Begum, signifies that she made the pilgrimage. All pilgrims who go to Mecca are allowed to add the word Haj to their names. The other word, Begum, indicates nobility, like the English title "Lady." Haji Begum is responsible for building her husband's

QUTB MINAR, *old postcard.* The Qutb Minar in New Delhi, India's capital, was built as a Tower of Victory. The construction of the 238-ft.-high tower was begun by the first Muslim sultan of Delhi, Qutb ud-Din, between 1193 and 1198, and completed by his successors.

tomb, which still stands in Delhi. With its spacious gardens and lofty dome, Humayun's beautiful tomb seems like a study for the later Taj Mahal.

When the Mughals arrived in Hindustan, the land was already ruled by Muslims. Within one hundred years of Muhammad's death, Islamic forces had conquered as far east as Sind, the westernmost part of Hindustan. Wave upon wave of Muslim invaders poured down upon Hindustan for centuries after that. Finally, in 1192, the Afghani ruler Muhammad Ghuri defeated the last Hindu king of Delhi, Raja Prithviraj. The center of Hindustan passed to Muslim control and the Sultanate of Delhi began.

Qutb ud-Din Aibak was Muhammad Ghuri's slave and general. Upon the king's death Qutb ud-Din proclaimed himself Sultan of Delhi and celebrated his new dynasty with the building of Delhi's first mosque. This mosque is known today as the *Quwwat-ul-Islam,* which means "The Might of Islam."

The mosque stands in ruins today, but it was a magnificent structure when it was built. It incorporated parts of Raja Prithviraj's destroyed Hindu temples. Next to it rose one of the wonders of the Muslim world, the Qutb Minar. This 238-foot-tall stone tower was a monument of victory to proclaim the triumph of Qutb ud-Din and his faith in the newly conquered land.

The Mughals entered Hindustan intent on fulfilling the duties of their religion. They did this throughout their history by building mosques, paying the salaries of Muslim clergy, and sending both pilgrims and vast sums of money to Mecca. Yet, as surely as it changed the way that they dressed and ate, this new land began to change their faith. In subtle ways their Muslim culture began to be influenced by the practices of the native Hindu tradition.

Some responded enthusiastically to this influence, but others resisted. At one extreme was the Emperor Akbar. He was curious and open-minded and questioned the rules of Islam in his search for the truth. His great-grandson Aurangzeb, however, was just the opposite. He was devoutly Muslim and sought to bring the empire back to its Islamic roots, away from the influence of Hindu thought.

It was only natural that this would happen in Hindustan. The land itself was permeated with the ancient Hindu belief. None who lived here could escape its influence. The very rivers were sacred, and the mountains holy. To the Hindus every rock and tree contained an essence of spirit, and there were many deities.

From the moment that they surveyed this new land, the Mughals, flush with victory, had to grapple with its heritage. Even more, they had to adjust to the climate and geography of the land itself. Hindustan, a formidable prize, was now theirs. This challenge brought them greatness.

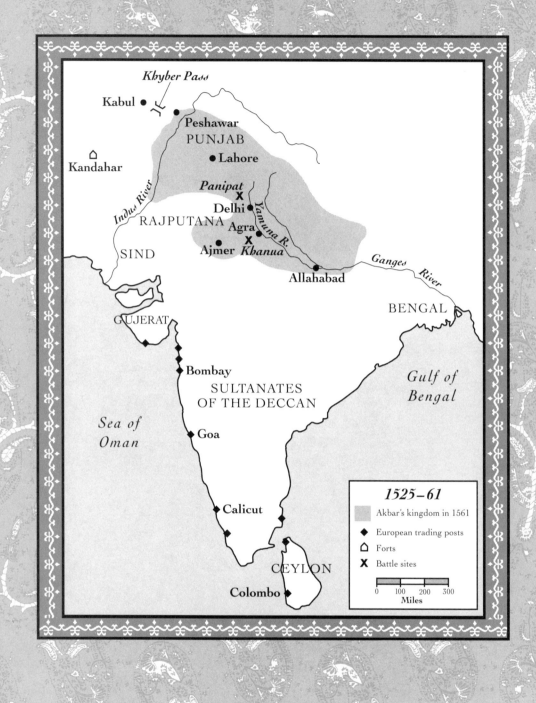

Kabul •

Khyber Pass

Kandahar △

Peshawar •

PUNJAB

Lahore •

Indus River

Panipat
✕

Delhi •

RAJPUTANA

Agra •
✕

Ajmer •
Khanua

Yamuna R.

SIND

Allahabad •

Ganges River

GUJERAT

BENGAL

Bombay ◆

*Sea of
Oman*

**SULTANATES
OF THE DECCAN**

Goa ◆

*Gulf of
Bengal*

Calicut ◆
◆

◆

CEYLON

Colombo ◆

1525–61

▨ Akbar's kingdom in 1561

◆ European trading posts

△ Forts

✕ Battle sites

0   100   200   300
Miles

Chapter 2

THE LAND

Hindustan . . . is a strange country. Compared to ours, it is another world. Its mountains, rivers, forests, and wildernesses, its villages and provinces, animals and plants, peoples and languages, even its rain and winds are altogether different.
— Baburnama

The New World

When Babur swept down into Hindustan he encountered a new world. It was a land unlike others, with strange wildlife, mysterious flowers, and fruits never before tasted.

It was April, the middle of the hot season. In Babur's Central Asian homeland, April was the end of winter's bitter cold and the beginning of springtime. Flowers began to bloom and the air was sweet and fresh. Not so in Hindustan. By April the air was filled with dust and blistering heat. Temperatures could soar as high as 116 degrees on the northern plains, and a hot, uncomfortable wind constantly blew. For lack of moisture everything withered in the excessive heat: the earth was parched, trees shed their leaves, and animals lay sapped of energy.

It was in this trying month that Babur took possession of Hindustan. When he arrived at Agra with his forces he took stock of their desperate situation.

THE EARLY MUGHAL EMPIRE AT THE BEGINNING OF AKBAR'S REIGN

When we came to Agra, it was the hot season, and the people all fled in fear. Neither grain for ourselves nor straw for our horses was to be found. The villages had been so plundered and pillaged that the people had turned to brigandage and thievery. The roads could not be traveled. . . . Also that year was very hot. Many began to sicken and die as though under the influence of a pestilent wind.

Things were so bad that Babur's commanders pressed him to turn around and flee Hindustan's deadly heat for the cool mountains of Afghanistan. He had barely arrived, and already Hindustan was putting Babur to the test. It would continue to challenge him to the end of his days.

Hindustan

Hindustan does not appear on contemporary maps. The land that Babur won has not been called by that name for many years. Ancient Hindustan now lies divided between the two modern countries of India and Pakistan. They were created in 1947 when the British gave independence to their immense crown colony of India.

The land that the Mughals called Hindustan centered on the northern regions of India and northeastern Pakistan. At the Mughal empire's height, it occupied territory that extended beyond the borders of that land. The former empire now lies in four modern states. Its mountainous northwestern lands are now part of Afghanistan, while its easternmost section lies in flat Bangladesh. One of the great Mughal imperial capitals, Lahore, now lies in Pakistan. The other two, Delhi and Agra, are located in India.

The most prominent feature of any map of South Asia is the Indian subcontinent, a vast triangle of land. At its southernmost point it resembles a thick finger hovering next to the island of Sri Lanka. Moving north the immense peninsula grows increasingly wide until it joins the Asian landmass at the Himalayas. This mountain range runs east to west for more than twenty-five hundred miles. It includes the world's highest summits: Mt. Everest at 29,028 feet and K-2 at 28,250. It also shelters Mt. Kailas, which is revered by the Hindus.

Although the Himalayas seemingly cut India's access to the rest of Asia, there has always been contact between the subcontinent and its neighboring lands. For thousands of years, invaders passed through the rugged northwestern mountains on their way to Hindustan. One of the last groups to use this route was the Mughals, led by Babur.

Two river systems, the Indus and the Ganges, flow through the plains at the base of the Himalayas. They were created by the unique weather pattern caused by these high mountains. Moisture-filled clouds heading northward from the seas are stopped by the mountains' immense wall. They are forced to release their moisture onto the peaks, which creates snow. The melting runoff flows downward into thousands of streams.

The Indus and its tributaries flow southwest from the mountains through present-day Pakistan. There they travel through parched lands and empty into the Arabian Sea. The oldest civilization on the subcontinent, the Harappa culture, centered on the Indus River. Near its banks archaeologists have excavated highly developed cities like Mohenjo Daro, dating from 2500 to 1500 B.C.E.

The Indus River is the source of the name Hindustan, which comes from Persian. According to A. L. Basham, author of *The Wonder That Was India,* the ancient Indians called this river the Sindhu, and in today's Pakistan the province that it flows through is called Sind. The Ancient Persians, however, had difficulty pronouncing the initial "S," and so they called it the Hindhu River. After Persia was conquered by Alexander the Great in 327 B.C.E., their word for the river passed on to the Greeks. The Greeks called the Indian landmass by the name of the Hindhu River. The Muslim world adopted this name for India. The land was called Hind, or Hindustan, meaning "land of the Hind people."

The ancient Indian language, Sanskrit, had its own names for the land. One was Jambudvipa, which means "the rose-apple island." At

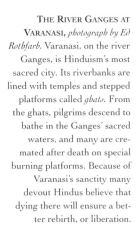

THE RIVER GANGES AT VARANASI, *photograph by Ed Rothfarb.* Varanasi, on the river Ganges, is Hinduism's most sacred city. Its riverbanks are lined with temples and stepped platforms called *ghats.* From the ghats, pilgrims descend to bathe in the Ganges' sacred waters, and many are cremated after death on special burning platforms. Because of Varanasi's sanctity many devout Hindus believe that dying there will ensure a better rebirth, or liberation.

its center, according to ancient myths, grew the immense jambu, or rose-apple tree. Another, taken from the name of a mythological emperor, was Bharatavarsa, or Bharata. The Puranas, a collection of old lore written down between 400 and 600 C.E., states: "The country that lies north of the ocean and south of the snowy mountains is called Bharata, for there dwell the descendants of Bharata."

Even in today's India, this ancient name is used to refer to the country. One of India's oldest cities, Varanasi, has an arts center at its Hindu University called the Bharat Kala Bhavan, which means the Bharat (or India) Arts Building.

Varanasi lies on the Ganges, which is India's most sacred river. *Ganga,* the river's name, is also that of the benevolent river goddess. Her sacred waters flow from the heavens onto the very head of Shiva, the great Hindu god. High upon Mount Kailas, his hallowed home, he breaks the water's fall, and, with his blessing, it flows downward to the plains. On its way east to the lush Bay of Bengal, the river flows through the heartland of India's classical culture.

This fertile plain was once called Aryavarta, the land of the

Aryans. These northern, light-skinned invaders began entering India from their homeland north of present-day Iran around 1500 B.C.E. The word *Iran* comes from the Aryans. They spoke a language that became the root for Sanskrit, India's classical language of religion and literature. Because Aryan peoples also invaded Europe, there are strong linguistic connections between India and Europe.

The swastika, the Nazi emblem, was an Aryan symbol for the sun-god. The word *swastika,* which became a symbol for oppression under the Nazis, derived from the Sanskrit word for "good luck." Indians neither approved nor condoned the use of their ancient symbol by the Nazis. Through the Nazis a hallowed sign of life became an emblem of hatred in the twentieth-century Western world.

The fierce Aryans destroyed the Harappan culture of the Indus River. They settled farther into the subcontinent, bringing their culture and religion. Their sacred work was called the Rg Veda, and the period that they ushered in has been named the Vedic age. During this long period, lasting into the middle of the first millenium B.C., the great sacred works of the Hindu religion were composed. Among these works was the *Mahabharata,* an epic tale of war comparable to the *Iliad* and *Odyssey* of Homer.

The north Indian plain, centered on the Ganges, was once highly fertile. Lush jungles filled the uncultivated land, but as the population increased, they were cut back. Time, deforestation, and poor farming techniques all contributed to depleting the once rich soil. Nevertheless this area boasts some of India's largest and oldest cities.

As the Ganges flows east, the land becomes more lush. This is the land of two rivers, where the Brahmaputra River flows down from Tibet. It joins the Ganges, and they fan out to create an immense delta emptying into the Bay of Bengal. This moist, fertile, province is also known as Bengal. Its flat lands have been cultivated with rice paddies from earliest times, and its people have always maintained their own distinct customs.

Today Bengal is shared between India and Bangladesh. In Mughal times it joined the empire under Akbar, who conquered it in

CASTE

The Aryans were responsible for introducing the roots of the caste system to India. Caste is one of the major elements of the Hindu religion. It assigns place and rank in society based on birth, and it exists to this day. When the light-skinned Aryan invaders encountered the darker-skinned native peoples of ancient India, they evolved a system of groupings in society called varnas, which means "colors." The system was both social and religious, so that highest-ranked varnas were most pure from a religious point of view.

All of society was divided into four main groups. The highest was the brahmin, traditionally the varna of priests. The second was the kshatriya, the warriors, nobles, and kings. The third was the vaishya, the merchants and farmers, and the fourth was the shudra, the varna of laborers and peasants. The highest ranks were the lightest skinned and the lowest, the darkest. Through Indian history the large varna groupings developed subgroups called jatis, which were both clan groupings, as in Scotland, and occupational groupings, as in guilds. There are literally thousands of

1576. Although it was one of the richest provinces in the empire, it was also one of the most troublesome. Mughal court chronicles were filled with talk of rebellions in Bengal, so far from the center of power in Agra. Bengal's riches encouraged corruption as well, and greedy imperial officers were often dismissed from their positions.

Between the Ganges plain and the western land of the Indus lies present day Rajasthan, once called Rajputana. Here the terrain shifts from the stark hills of the Aravalli Range into semi-arid plains and finally the sandy wastes of the Thar Desert. This land has always sheltered the many kingdoms of the Rajput clans, fierce Hindu warriors whose castles still dominate the region's cities.

these jatis today, and the word "caste" comes from the Portuguese term for these jatis.

Below all four of these was another group. They were outside of the system and therefore shunned by the rest of society. They were given the tasks that were considered the most impure from a religious point of view, like cleaning lavatories or sweeping. This group was given the name harijan, meaning "children of God," by Mahatma Gandhi, the great leader of twentieth-century India. Gandhi saw the oppression of the caste system, in which everyone's position in society was rigidly defined by their birth, not their abilities. He was an inspiration for the African-American leader Dr. Martin Luther King, Jr., and his struggle for civil rights in America.

Today the Constitution of India protects the harijans, whom it calls the "scheduled castes," from discrimination. It offers them guaranteed places in the government service and schools, much like affirmative-action legislation in the United States. In both countries as well, there are conflicts over these laws, and the issue is debated as much in the Indian Parliament as it is in the United States Congress.

The Rajputs lived for honor, and their code dictated fighting unto death. When defeat was certain, their women performed the rite of *jauhar*, burning themselves alive rather than submitting to dishonor. During Emperor Akbar's 1567 siege of the great Rajput fort of Chittorgarh, the commander of the fort was killed by the emperor himself. Shortly after that happened, smoke began to rise from the besieged fortress. It was the flames of the noble Rajput ladies who were committing ritual suicide by fire. The death of their commander signaled imminent defeat, and for them *jauhar* was the only honorable alternative.

The Rajputs were formidable warriors, but their primary allegiance was to their own group. Like the proud clans of Scotland, they often fought among themselves and were seldom able to form a united front against invaders. Yet from the time of Akbar on, the Mughals realized that a stable empire depended on strong alliances with these skilled fighters. Akbar married a Rajput princess and their son Prince Salim succeeded Akbar as Emperor Jahangir. From then on, the Mughal emperors had Rajput blood flowing in their veins.

Leading south from the northern plain and Rajasthan is a highland area that culminates in the Vindhya Mountains. This low range has formed the historic boundary between north and south India. All the land above this range, as far as the Himalaya Mountains, was traditionally called Hindustan. Once Mughals were in full control of the north, they turned their attention south toward the unconquered region below the mountains, the Deccan.

Deccan means "south." Under Akbar's successors, this area became the most sought after addition to the empire, and the most frustrating. The heart of the Deccan is a dry and hilly plateau. Some of its landscape resembles the moon's, with huge boulders and deep depressions. On either side the Deccan is separated from the lush coasts by two ranges of hills, and most of the region remains dry.

Despite this there were a number of wealthy kingdoms in the Deccan. The area possessed great mineral wealth, and Golconda, in the central southeast, was once the world center for the diamond trade. The small size of the Deccan kingdoms made them tempting targets for Mughal ambitions. Starting with Akbar, and then under the determined Emperor Aurangzeb, the conquest of the Deccan was accomplished, and the Mughal empire reached its greatest size. The triumph was shortlived, for after Aurangzeb's death the empire quickly fell into decline, and the Deccan soon broke free.

On India's two coasts, palm trees fringe the topaz waters. In Mughal times these idyllic shores already harbored the tiny European settlements that grew to be India's ultimate threat. By the time of Babur's conquest in 1525, the Portuguese had made settlements on both coasts. These settlements, at Goa, Daman, Diu, and Hughli, were set up for both trade and territorial expansion.

The Mughals cared little for overseas trade, for in most things they were self-sufficient. They liked European art and baubles but were not interested in trading alliances. The Europeans, by contrast, desperately wanted access to Hindustan's gems, spices, and finished goods, particularly its superior textiles. They took advantage of the late Mughal Empire's disintegration to gradually conquer portions of the subcontinent.

The British grabbed the lion's share. By the nineteenth century, India had become the crown jewel of their world empire. Yet, in the end, they too departed, the last in a long line of conquerors.

The Climate

Next to geography, India's unique climate plays the most critical role in shaping its peoples' lives. The vast land has various climates in its far-flung regions, but certain elements dominate the entire subcontinent. There are three basic seasons: the cool season from October to late February; the hot season from late February to May; and the wet season from late May until September. The passage from the rigors of the hot season, which Babur experienced on his arrival, to the relief of the wet one is by far the most significant in the entire year.

India's northern plains, the Mughals' Hindustan, suffer most in the hot season. Starting in March the dry heat mounts until June, when the land itself appears to die. François Bernier, the French physician at the Mughal court, described the life during this time:

> The heat is so intense . . . that no one, not even the king, wears stockings; the only covering for the feet being *babouches*, or slippers. . . . During the summer seasons it is scarcely possible to keep the hand on the wall of an apartment, or the head in a pillow. For more than six successive months everybody lies in the open air without covering—

the common people in the streets, the merchants and persons of condition . . . in their courts or gardens, and sometimes on their terraces, which are first carefully watered.

Sometime in June the clouds begin to appear. Powerful heat radiating upward from the land draws moisture inland from the seas. The clouds turn dark, and thick banks roll inward toward the land. The wind picks up, lightning flashes, and the sky fills with the crash of thunder and releases huge torrents of rain. The monsoon has finally arrived.

This is a time of great joy, for the dry, dusty heat has been banished until the following year. Babur particularly enjoyed the monsoon.

> The weather turns very nice during the monsoon. Sometimes it rains ten, fifteen, or twenty times a day; torrents are formed in an instant, and water flows in places that normally have no water. . . . The weather is unusually good when the rain ceases, so good in fact that it could not be more temperate or pleasant.

The word *monsoon* derives from the word *mausim,* which means "season" in both Arabic and Hindi. It is a special time for Hindustan's people. The dark clouds, lightning, and thunder that terrify the people of other cultures symbolize joy and abundance for them. Their tradition speaks of the blessed "voice" of the thunder. It is no coincidence that the Hindu god *Krishna's* birthday is celebrated in August, the time of the monsoon.

In the miracle of the monsoon, the land turns green overnight, trees put out new leaves, and wildlife returns. Like springtime in other lands, *this* is the season of rebirth. The crops are sown and in celebration of the land's fertility, weddings are celebrated.

Despite the joy, the monsoon season often brings problems. Major flooding occurs and travel can be difficult. Mughal emperors going to battle tried to avoid this season for their campaigns. Those who couldn't, like the Emperor Humayun, met with disaster. This is also the traditional time for epidemics, when waterborne diseases thrive. Nevertheless, the life-giving rains are eagerly awaited by all.

By early autumn the rains have diminished, and the fields are filled with crops. Days sparkle with warm, sunny weather, and the harvest is gathered. This is the time of festivals, when the great Hindu holidays of Durga Puja and Diwali are celebrated.

The northern plains experience a mild winter, with cool nights and dry, sunny days. People wrap up in shawls to protect themselves from the winds blowing down from the icy Himalayas. Even the elephants suffer in the cold. One brisk winter morning, the Emperor Jahangir noticed his elephants shivering as they were being washed. When he realized that the cold water was adding to their discomfort, he ordered that their bathing water be heated during the winter from then on.

By winter's end, in late February, there is a brief, transitional spring-like period before the onset of the hot season. The days are pleasant and delicate flowers briefly bloom. This was the time for the greatest of the Mughal court celebrations, the Persian New Year, called Nauroz. The Emperor Akbar introduced this celebration during his reign, with magnificent parties, fireworks, and gift-giving that lasted for up to eighteen days. By the end of Nauroz, the ferocious heat started to build, and everyone pined for the return of the monsoon.

The Religion

During the lush rains of the monsoon, Hindus in parts of northern India celebrate Krishna Janmashtami, the birth of the god Krishna. Everyone's home has been cleaned and specially decorated, and all have fasted the entire day until midnight, the moment of the god's birth. At that time, little statues of the baby god, much like Jesus' image at Christmas, are lovingly placed in cradles, worshiped, and ceremoniously bathed. Stories are told of the god's miraculous birth,

THE WHITE BULL NANDI AND SHIVA, *poster. Collection of Ed Rothfarb.* All major Hindu gods are associated with an animal who is their "mount." The god Shiva's mount is Nandi the great white bull that Shiva rides into battle. The bull represents power, and many Shiva temples have a large sculpture of Nandi facing reverently toward Shiva's sanctuary. Bulls and cows have been sacred to Hindus since ancient times.

and special pageants called *Krishnalila* are performed. Krishna's favorite foods are eaten as well. They are all dairy foods, for legends depict this beloved god as a handsome cowherd.

Krishna's skin is the beautiful blue of rain-bearing clouds. He symbolizes the eternal link between Nature, Hindustan's land, and her people's deep faith. Their religion centers on their land, which they hold to be sacred. Their mountains are the abode of gods, and their rivers the home of goddesses. Every part of nature both great and small is potentially holy. Even snakes are worshiped, and the gentle cow is revered as a symbol of fertility and abundance.

The Hindu philosophy of life developed from their early sages' perceptions of divine Nature. They saw that their gods could make the land abundant but then destroy that bounty with quick, savage force. Their land witnessed forces of creation and destruction continually playing against each other. The extremes of climate, the earthquakes, and constant invasions made them feel that reality was not fixed and permanent. Even Babur noted this unique feature of Hindustan: "In Hindustan the destruction and building of villages, hamlets, even of cities, can be accomplished in an instant." With this sense of constant change came the idea that this world is not really the true world. The sages reasoned that if a flower lives only to wither and die, and whole villages can be washed away by the monsoon's floods, then there must be a more powerful, eternal force than the one that we see in our everyday lives. They felt that everything that we see and touch in this world—buildings, animals, food, and friends—is only an illusion. They called this illusion *maya*. For them the only true reality was based within, where the eternal spirit, called *atman*, dwelt. Their highest goal was to learn about this other, truer internal reality. To help them toward this goal, they prayed, meditated, and followed spiritual practices designed to focus them on the interior world.

The early Hindu sages saw time differently than we do in the modern West. Our calendars, for instance, are based on a concept of time that is centered on the birth of Jesus. All years in our calendar are designated either B.C., before Jesus' birth, or A.D., after. Another of our systems uses the same time frame but designates the divisions as B.C.E. (Before the Common Era) and C.E. (Common Era). The Hindu sages thought of time in terms of vast cycles, eras that repeated through eternity. They saw that each year the land dies and bursts forth anew with the life-giving rains. Everything changes and then repeats yet again. These cycles are like wheels endlessly spinning through time.

To Hindus, the greatest cycle is so vast that humans can barely comprehend it. It is the cycle of the life of *Brahma*, the creator god. His life lasts for one hundred Brahmanic years, and each year equals three hundred eleven trillion, forty billion (311,040,000,000,000) human years. By comparison the lives of human beings are infinitesimal cycles. Hindu sages believe that lives and deaths repeat endlessly through time. At death the spirit travels into a new life, only to live, die, and then be reborn once again.

The highest destiny that one can achieve is to leave this endlessly repeating cycle, but it takes many, many lifetimes. The only way to leave the continuously spinning wheel of rebirths is to strive for good *karma*. Karma is the law of actions and their effects. Good actions bring rebirths into better lives. This is accomplished through devotions, prayers, and right living. With enough good karma accumulated through many lifetimes, one can finally be liberated from the wheel of rebirth. This is called *moksha*.

The Gods

The world of the Hindu gods reflects the sages' perceptions of life. The gods represent the forces of creation and destruction that dominate the world. Some gods create, some destroy, and yet others do both. The quality unique to Hinduism is that creation and destruction are not thought of as good or evil, but rather as fundamental, ever-present parts of life. They are two sides of the same coin, and the coin is forever spinning.

The gods are everywhere. Like the gods of Greek and Roman mythology, many Hindu gods have human characteristics, and they have marvelous adventures. Gods fight in battles, fall in love, and teach mankind important lessons. Like the Greek and Roman gods as well, the Hindu gods can transform themselves into different beings, and some of their most wonderful tales involve these extraordinary feats. But unlike the other gods, the many Hindu deities are ultimately expressions of the one true universal spirit.

The two greatest male gods are Vishnu the Preserver and Shiva the Destroyer and Creator. As the preserver god, Vishnu watches over everything that keeps the universe running in good order. Anything that helps to run the world—laws, the structure of society, the family—is under the domain of Vishnu. He is the guardian of humanity and the protector of the *dharma,* the cosmic order of the universe. Since Vishnu preserves society, he is associated with rulers, whose job it is to rule society. He is also associated with caste, for this is the way society was ordered.

Besides his regal role as protector of society, Vishnu has ten other forms, called *avatars.* One of them is the heroic king Rama, whose epic tale is called the *Ramayana.* Another, very different one is the god Matsya, who is shaped like a fish.

None of his avatars is as beloved as Krishna, the blue-colored god. Krishna is a warrior, a prince posing as a sacred cowherder, and a divine lover. He is the ally of humanity, and his playful exploits are cherished by his devotees. The region of his birth lay near the Mughals' capital at Agra. It was called Braj, and there, under the Mughals, some great Hindu nobles constructed temples in Krishna's honor. Some were even built with gifts of money from the Muslim Mughal emperors.

The great god Shiva is the opposite of Krishna. Shiva's name means "the Auspicious One," and he represents the continuing creation and destruction of the universe. He is an aloof god, and he is often depicted far removed from humanity, sitting on his tiger skin atop Mt. Kailas, deep in meditation. Shiva is also called Nataraja, the "Lord of the Dance." He performs his eternal dance to a drum beat that is said to be the rhythm of the universe itself. While other gods are depicted as beautiful humans, Shiva is often represented in the form of an abstract phallic symbol, the *linga.*

Both Vishnu and Shiva have female consorts, and they are very present in the world. Shiva's consort has many forms. In her protective, kindly aspect she is the beautiful goddess known as Sati or Parvati, the ideal wife and mother. In her darker aspects she is worshiped as Durga, a powerful warrior goddess, or Kali, who wears a necklace of skulls.

These are all forms of the great goddess, known simply as Devi.

IMAGES OF HINDUISM

KRISHNA, *poster. Collection of Ed Rothfarb.* Krishna is one of the ten avatars, or forms, of the great god Vishnu. There are many legends about Krishna, but the most beloved depict him as a beautiful, princely young cowherder in the countryside. Here he is shown playing his flute with a cow and her calf. Krishna is adorned with jewels, as befits both a prince and a god.

SHIVA AND PARVATI,
photograph by Ed Rothfarb.
In Hinduism the balance of divine male and female energy is very important, and many of the chief male gods have female consorts. Here a folk wall painting in a village shows Shiva and his consort Parvati standing in a lotus blossom.

KANDARIYA MAHADEVA HINDU TEMPLE AT KHAJU-RAHO. *Photograph courtesy the American Institute of Indian Studies, Varanasi.*
This carved stone Hindu temple was built at Khajuraho, in central India, around the year A.D. 1050 by the Chandella dynasty. It is one of the most beautiful examples of the northern India Hindu temple "carved mountain" style. The exterior walls are covered with thousands of graceful statues of the gods and their attendants, all carved from stone.

The ancient mother goddess, called Mata, is associated with the earth and its great rivers, like the Ganges. As the mother she nourishes and provides for her worshipers, but her other aspect is dark, the bringer of death and disease. Like the earth, with which she is associated, Devi simultaneously sustains and destroys mankind.

The world of the gods is full of legends and tales. Their exploits are engagingly human, like the baby Krishna stealing sweet butter to eat, or Ganesh, the elephant-headed god, guarding his mother Parvati's chamber. To this day many Hindus worship their gods as sculpted images, which are bathed, dressed, offered food, and put to bed at night—just as one would a beloved child. This is one way of showing reverence for the spirit of the deity, which, Hindus believe, comes to dwell in the image.

One of the most important acts of worship is called *darshan*. At certain times of day, the shrine of the deity is opened. The worshiper looks directly at the god's prominent, open eyes. Hindus believe that at that moment the god is looking directly back at them. This idea of viewing a great figure has also been used for political ends by Hindustan's rulers. The Mughal emperors used it in their daily ceremony of appearing to the public. Each day at sunrise, the emperors appeared at a window in their palace called the *Jharoka-i Darshan*, and showed themselves to the people assembled below. This was one way that Hindu practices came to influence the Mughal emperors.

Yet the practice of darshan could not be further from the core of orthodox Muslim belief. The world of Islam worshiped one god, not many, and the worship of images was absolutely forbidden. Muhammad had destroyed all idols as false gods. Now in Hindustan the Muslims lived among a Hindu majority who worshiped idols every day. The two faiths were totally different.

Two Differing Beliefs

Islam and Hinduism were separated not only by their beliefs but by their practices. Muslims worshiped in mosques that were built to accommodate large congregations for prayer. Their mosques had no statues or painted images of people or animals. None had an altar. Instead there was a decoratively embellished niche called the *mihrab*, which indicated the *qibla*, or direction of worship. In orthodox Islam no music accompanied worship, no incense was burned, nor were flowers offered. This was a religion born in the stark simplicity of the desert.

Hindus, by contrast, worshiped in temples that swarmed inside and out with carved, painted images. Their small temples resembled sculpted mountains. Within their dark, cavelike interiors lived the images of the gods, reverenced amid the sweet smells of incense, the color of flowers, food, and the glowing flames of many lamps. Chants, drums, and bells accompanied the worship, and sometimes sacred dance as well. Statues were carried around the sanctuaries and out into the streets in colorful, noisy processions thronged with believers.

Muslims ate no pork but enjoyed beef, lamb, and goat. Hindus, on the other hand, held the cow sacred, and many were vegetarians. Muslim clergy kept their heads covered and dressed in long robes. Hindu priests traditionally wore nothing above their waists except a sacred string. Muslims visited their saints' tombs in Hindustan, but their greatest pilgrimage was to far-off Mecca, toward which they prayed daily. Hindus, by contrast, made pilgrimages only within Hindustan, visiting its countless shrines.

These two religions finally met when Muslim forces conquered Hindustan late in the twelfth century. That encounter was painful for the Hindu population. Many of their temples were destroyed, and discriminatory taxes were settled on them. Yet for low-caste Hindus and harijans, Islam offered a religion that saw all people as equals, no matter what their caste. With the arrival of the new faith, some Hindus converted, and today their numerous descendants populate Pakistan, Bangladesh, and much of India. Since the time of the Muslim conquests, Hindus and Muslims have had a mixed, complex history in Hindustan. The two communities generally lived peaceful but separate lives. Their relationship was like a slow pendulum that swung back and forth between harmony and discord.

By Mughal times the two faiths had lived together on Hindustan's soil for more than three hundred years. Despite their vast differences, their close proximity fostered gradual exchanges. A new language called Urdu developed that mixed Hindi and Persian words and was written in Persian script. Today Urdu is the official language of Pakistan.

Influenced by Hindu social customs, Muslims actually adopted a mild form of caste in some areas of India. Devotional music was sung in Muslim shrines, and some Hindu temples began to exhibit the influence of Muslim architecture. Upper-class Hindus were also influenced by Muslim social customs, and they began practicing *purdah*, the seclusion of women. Finally, in the early 1500s a new faith was born on Indian soil that combined Hindu and Muslim teachings. This was the Sikh religion founded by Guru Nanak (1469–1539). Today Sikhs constitute only two percent of India's population, but they are an important community.

The Mughal era witnessed the greatest flowering of these exchanges. Akbar was responsible for initiating many of them, and part of his greatness as a ruler lay in his willingness to draw on the talents of both communities. During his reign many Hindus joined the largely Muslim imperial administration, and members of both faiths mixed at court. One of the great cultural achievements of Akbar's reign was the translation of Hindu epics such as the *Mahabharata* from their original Sanskrit into Persian. Teams of Muslim and Hindu translators worked together to produce these new texts, and they were beautifully illustrated by court painters of both faiths.

Akbar's great-grandson, the scholarly Prince Dara Shikoh, took this exchange one step further with his book *The Mingling of the Two*

Oceans. In it he attempted to reconcile the differences between the two faiths by showing their shared philosophic roots. Although Akbar would have been proud of his achievement, the unfortunate prince lived in far more conservative times. In the course of a struggle for the throne, Dara Shikoh was condemned as a religious heretic and executed. His brother, the Emperor Aurangzeb, restored the discriminatory measures against Hindus that Akbar had removed, and the pendulum swung backward again.

Today, relations between Hindus and Muslims in India are still troubled. Perhaps the deepest indication of these problems was the destruction in 1992 of a mosque at Ayodhya in northern India. The Hindu extremists who destroyed the mosque claimed that it had been built on the site of a previously destroyed temple dedicated to their god Rama. After the mosque's destruction, a wave of religious violence followed in which many people were killed. The foundations of religious harmony so carefully nurtured by India's Constitution faced their gravest threat since Independence.

The destroyed mosque was known as the Babri Masjid, the Mosque of Babur. It was built by a nobleman from the court of Babur in the late 1520s, after his lord achieved the greatest victory of his life, the conquest of Hindustan.

The Mughal adventure began with Babur, and for generations after he would be venerated by his Imperial descendants. After his death he was given the exalted Persian title *Ferdaus Makani*, which meant "placed in Heaven." Babur's tale started out in a land that was more than one thousand miles distant from his final capital in Hindustan. It was distant in all respects: its people looked different, they spoke a strange language, and their culture bore no relation to that of Hindustan. Yet, by the end of his life, Babur laid claim to this vast foreign land.

His adventure started in a tiny Central Asian kingdom, worlds away from the utter splendor that his descendants would attain.

Chapter 3

ZAHIR UD-DIN MUHAMMAD BABUR

ZAHIR UD-DIN MUHAMMAD BABUR

A Prince from Central Asia

The story of Babur's life reads like mythology or the King Arthur legend. A young prince descended from royalty grew up in a land of small kingdoms perpetually at war. His greatest dream was to restore the once-glorious empire of his ancestors, but misfortune struck and the prince lost all. With no home left and little money, he was forced to lead a wandering life. As he traveled he had many exciting adventures, but he never gave up his lifelong quest for his own kingdom.

He was just, learned, and courageous. Because of his admirable qualities he attracted many followers who joined his cause. Finally, after hard work and many disappointments, his extraordinary destiny came to pass. He won a splendid new empire, even greater than his glorious ancestor's, and founded a magnificent dynasty.

This story was true, and the storyteller none other than the prince himself, Zahir ud-Din Muhammad Babur. Babur, whose name means "the Tiger," lived from 1483 until 1530. Throughout his years of struggle and adventure, he jotted notes and kept diaries. Later in

YURT, *1909, photograph by Sergei Mikhailovich Prokudin-Gorskii. Library of Congress, Washington, D.C.* The yurt is the typical dwelling of the Turkic-Mongolian nomads of Central Asia. Babur's nomadic warrior cousins would have lived in structures like these, and even today some Mongolians live in yurts.

life, when finally he had won his empire, he wrote his story in Chagatay Turkish, his native tongue. In 1589, during the reign of his grandson, the great Mughal Emperor Akbar, the story was translated into Persian. It was called the *Baburnama*, the Book of Babur, and through this work his incredible life has come down to us.

Babur was a young prince when an unexpected turn of events changed his life: "In the month of Ramadan, in the year 899 (June of 1494), in the province of Ferghana, in my twelfth year I became king."

He grew up in late-fifteenth-century Central Asia, a vast area more than a thousand miles from Hindustan. Central Asia lies north of the Himalayas. His region, Transoxiana, was the land of the Oxus River. The Oxus runs southeast from the Aral Sea into deserts. Today much of this area lies in the republics of Uzbekistan and Tadjikistan, once part of the Soviet Union.

Central Asia is a harsh, dry land sweeping all the way from the Caspian Sea to the Chinese border. A shallow desert basin, almost half the size of the continental United States, its northern border is grassy uplands. To the south and east lie the forbidding Pamir and Tien Shan mountain ranges. Because of its rough geography, only certain areas could be settled and cultivated. Transoxiana, between two rivers, was one of these areas. It lay astride major caravan routes to China, the West, and Hindustan, and had developed prosperous cities.

The region suffers tremendous extremes of climate: freezing winters and scorching summers. Winds are fierce and earthquakes frequent. Rainfall is scarce, and water is as preciously guarded as gold. Irrigation and careful management of water resources was the only way that agriculture could survive. It was also key to cultivating the gardens that Babur treasured.

In the late fifteenth century, the people of Transoxiana were as divided as was its climate. The plains and grasslands, called steppes, were inhabited by nomadic tribes who were Turkic and Mongol in origin. They migrated with their herds from their lowland winter pastures to the summer's grassy highlands. They lived in round tents called *yurts*, and were organized into clans headed by chiefs called *amirs* or *begs*. Babur's distinguished ancestor Timur had the title Amir Timur, signifying that he was a clan chief. These tribes were Muslim, like most of Central Asia, but had only converted at the beginning of the fourteenth century. Prior to that their ancient, pre-Islamic beliefs included reliance on *shamans*, tribal ritual healers. These nomads disdained people who followed a settled agricultural life or, even worse, who lived in cities.

The city dwellers in turn considered the nomads to be complete barbarians. This is not surprising since Central Asia's cities were among the world's most civilized. Within their walls, amid beautiful surroundings, nobles lived lives of great refinement, scholars taught in the many colleges, and merchants filled bazaars with treasures.

Persian: The International Culture

From top to bottom, the prevailing urban culture was Persian, and Persian was the language of government. Muslim religious education was conducted in Arabic, so that educated Central Asians knew at least three languages, Persian, Arabic, and their own tongue. Persian speakers dominated the cities, as well as the settled countryside.

Persian culture derived from the ancient land of Persia, an area far larger than today's Iran. By Babur's time Persian culture was completely international and stretched thousands of miles, from eastern Syria to points near China. The culture was based on language and values shared by an international elite. Just as people throughout the world now use English on the Internet or to discuss science or business, Persian was *the* language for Central Asia's educated peoples.

Classical Persian was a refined language, perfect for diplomacy and literature. All who learned it read great classics like the *Shahnama*, the eleventh-century "Book of Kings." It was written by the poet Firdausi and offered marvelous legends of Persia's ancient rulers. Historical writing was also prized in this world, as were certain sciences and astronomy. Some of the great classics of the Greco-Roman world had been translated into Persian, and this knowledge was widely used.

Poetry was the most exalted form of literature, and many of the elite composed verses. Babur himself wrote poetry in both Persian and his native Turkish. Some of Central Asia's rulers were accomplished poets, among them Sultan Husain Baiqara, Babur's distant relative. His court in the city of Herat was the most important artistic center of late-fifteenth-century Central Asia.

Painting was almost as prized as poetry, but while many aristocrats wrote poetry, few painted. Painting was practiced by artisans whose families had traditionally practiced the same craft. Rulers maintained studios of painters at their courts. Babur's descendants, the Mughals, would become leading patrons of this art.

The Ruling Class

Babur once visited his clan relations who were still living a nomadic lifestyle on the steppes. His memories of that visit showed the gulf between them. The young prince, heir to a noble, long-settled family, was appalled at his uncle's tent. He wrote that it "looked like a robber's den — melons and grapes and horse trappings strewn all over." Despite the differences that separated the princely elite from the clans, they were still bound by strong ties.

Time and again fierce nomadic invaders wound up settling the rich lands they conquered. Babur's own ancestors had followed this pattern. The Mongol invasions of the thirteenth century caused widespread slaughter and destruction throughout Central Asia. Yet, within generations, the fierce Mongols had joined the settled elites. The ferocious invaders who had inspired terror in half of Asia were now devout Muslims, composed Persian poetry, and patronized their court artists.

Babur was descended from both peoples. On his mother's side his ancestor was the feared Mongol invader Jenghiz Khan (Genghis Khan), while his father was the great-great-grandson of the Turk Amir Timur. As the two peoples blended, Amir Timur married a daughter of Jenghiz Khan and took the Mongolian title of Kürägän, meaning "son-in-law." The Persianized form of this word was *Gurkan,* and hundreds of years later, the Mughal dynasty, proud of its descent from Amir Timur, would call their dynasty by this name, "Gurkani."

TIMUR HANDING THE IMPER-
IAL CROWN TO BABUR,
*ca. 1630, by Govardhan. Courtesy
the Board of Trustees, Victoria and
Albert Museum, London.*
Amir Timur, the great ancestor
of the Mughals, hands the
crown to Babur, the founder
of the dynasty. On the right is
Babur's son Humayun. Shah
Jahan commissioned this symbolic painting to depict his lineage. Timur died seventy-eight
years before Babur was born,
and Humayun was only
twenty-three years old when
Babur died.

Amir Timur, who lived from 1336 to 1405, grew up in Central Asia, became its ruler, and launched numerous expeditions of conquest throughout Asia. In 1398 he invaded Hindustan and brought back extraordinary wealth. Through his many conquests, he established a strong and wealthy empire centered on his capital at Samarqand. After his death the empire broke up into smaller kingdoms ruled by his descendants, including his great-grandson Umar-Shaykh Mirza, the father of Babur. Because of their link to Timur, these are called Timurid kingdoms, and the Mughals, to this day, are sometimes referred to as Timurids.

The cycle of invasion and settlement was in full force in Babur's time. His early life was dominated by fierce new invaders who ejected him from his homeland. These were the Uzbeks, a Turkic-Mongol people from north of Transoxiana. Led by their skillful commanding prince, Shaybani Khan, they gradually conquered so much of Amir Timur's former empire that Babur was the only descendant left with a kingdom. The Uzbeks conquered Transoxiana so thoroughly that part of the region is now called Uzbekistan, the land of the Uzbeks.

All of the princes descended from Amir Timur had the same vision. They dreamt of restoring the glory of their ancestor's former empire, yet none were strong enough to accomplish it. In the ambitious quest to enlarge their territories, they waged constant war against each other. Duels and revenge killings were frequent. Carrying an enemy's severed head as a trophy was not uncommon, nor was building piles of heads after a battle. It was against this rich but turbulent backdrop that Babur came into the world.

Babur's Origins

Babur was born on February 14, 1483, and grew up in Ferghana, the valley that was his family's kingdom. Ferghana lay to the east of the great city of Samarqand. According to Babur it was smallish, surrounded by mountains on three sides, and fertile. The Jaxartes River flowed right through the valley, which enabled Ferghana to produce ample grain and fruit.

From his descriptions it seemed like a happy place, filled with beautiful landscapes and rugged mountains for adventure. It was happy as well because there was abundant water, which Babur considered crucial for a civilized life. In Central Asia, with its vast deserts, water was life itself. Throughout his life Babur would try to re-create the peace and pleasure of his childhood home by building gardens.

His memoirs began with a description of his home and father, Umar-Shaykh Mirza. Umar-Shaykh was the ruler of Ferghana, and as Amir Timur's direct descendant he bore the noble title of Mirza, meaning "Prince." Babur, the firstborn son, was one of eight children. Only Babur and his sister Khanzada Begum were full siblings. The rest were born of the Shaykh's other consorts.

Babur's mother, Qutlugh Nigar Khanim, was the direct descendant of Jenghiz Khan. As a result her son had a doubly distinguished ancestry, an important factor in his future career. Furthermore, the throne of Ferghana would one day be his, as the firstborn son. That day came sooner than expected.

Umar-Shaykh Mirza Becomes a Falcon

Babur's father, Umar-Shaykh Mirza, was not an imposing figure, despite his illustrious ancestry. According to his son he was "short in stature, had a round beard and a fleshy face, and was fat. He wore his tunic so tight that to fasten the ties, he had to hold in his stomach; if he let himself go it often happened that the ties broke." Babur was a dutiful son and thought highly of his father, who, though "unceremonious in both dress and speech," was devout, good-natured, just, and eloquent. Babur's own disregard for putting on airs was no doubt inherited from his down-to-earth father. Umar-Shaykh might have been careless in his appearance, but he was well-read. Like many Central Asian aristocrats, he even had a talent for poetry.

As a proper, though somewhat down-at-the-heels, ruler, Umar-Shaykh strove to add glory to his reign. Unlike other princes, who were bound to an overlord, he was an independent ruler, a *padshah*, which Babur considered highly significant. By his son's twelfth year, Umar-Shaykh had already made several unsuccessful attempts to expand his tiny kingdom. A number of them were aimed at conquering Samarqand from his brother, Sultan Ahmad-Mirza. But before the thirty-nine-year-old ruler could attempt any more, "a strange event occurred," as Babur put it, which ended his life.

Umar-Shaykh's fortress at Akshi was perched high atop a cliff. Far below flowed the Jaxartes River, while deep ravines surrounded the walls. Built into the walls, and overlooking a precipice, was a small dovecote, or birdhouse. There Umar-Shaykh would often come to relax by flying his treasured pigeons. One day, while visiting the dove house, the ground gave way beneath him. All of a sudden, in Babur's poetic words, he "flew from the ravine with his doves and dovecote and became a falcon." Plummeting into the depths of the ravine, Umar-Shaykh met his death.

The twelve-year-old prince was visiting a garden one day's journey away when urgent news reached him of the accident. He rushed back to Akshi, but, convinced that the boy was in danger, his father's loyal adviser sent him away to the highland's relative safety.

Ferghana Threatened

A small kingdom ruled by a child was a powerful temptation for ambitious princes intent on expansion. Familial relations were no guarantee of peace. One's greatest enemies could often be greedy uncles or jealous brothers who craved the same throne.

Rulers achieved conquest by attracting local clans and their leaders to their service. These fighters were the military backbone, without whom a ruler was powerless. Much like medieval Europe, where feudal lords led their liege men into battle, Transoxiana's princes went forth to battle at the head of their clans. Like medieval Europeans as well, its princes ruled from hilltop fortresses protected by moats. Even little Ferghana boasted a number of them.

Followers came for the prestige of serving a powerful lord, and for the promise of loot. Each group joined or declined as it saw fit. They were notoriously fickle and were not above changing sides if they sensed that better rewards might come their way. They also deserted, and in Babur's early years this was a major problem.

When he captured Samarqand for the first time, the city was impoverished, but his troops were expecting their booty.

> We were in no position to give them anything. Thinking of their homes, they began to desert one by one and two by two. The first to desert was Khan-Quli Buyan-Quli, and then Ibrahim Begchik. The Moghuls all deserted. Later even Sultan-Ahmad Tambal deserted.

With problems like this to contend with, the fortunes of Transoxiana's princes rose and fell with astonishing frequency. At this moment young Babur's fortune appeared particularly bleak. Two invading forces were preparing to wrest Ferghana away from him, but as luck would have it, they failed. A flooded river carried away many of the invader's steeds, an epidemic did in the rest, and then both commanders fell ill.

The grateful prince attributed it all to a higher power.

> God, who by his perfect power has brought to fruition . . . every labor of mine . . . effected a few events that caused them not merely to change their minds about coming but actually to regret having set out.

Now he could regroup and focus on the quest that was to occupy the better part of his life. Babur looked around him and saw the shambles of a once-great empire, like a broken crown. What nobler quest could there be than restoring it to glory? The first step was to possess its crown jewel, Samarqand. To a boy from a poor, small province, there was no greater dream than conquering the fairest city in the world.

The Dream of Samarqand

Glorious Samarqand was Timur's former imperial capital. While nomadic tents, mud-baked hill towns, and crude fortresses dotted Central Asia's rugged landscape, its polished metropolis was an entirely different world. "The city of Samarqand is an amazingly ornamented city," Babur enthused. Within rose noble mosques. Their swelling domes, covered with tiles of turquoise as brilliant as sparkling water, could be seen for miles around. Graceful minarets towered over the mosques while beautiful patterns of brightly colored tiles emblazoned prayers on their facades.

The Turks and Mongols called it Semizkand, "Fat City," an allusion to its wealth. It had been enriched immeasurably by Timur, who brought spoils back from his far-ranging conquests. There he brought the greatest artists of his day and craftsmen from all across Asia to build its fabled buildings. Babur wrote of one impressive mosque built entirely by stonemasons from Hindustan. At the city's heart lay the main square, the Registan. From there, main streets—flanked on three sides by magnificent mosques and *madrasas*, Muslim colleges—radiated outward to the six city gates.

Within Samarqand's walls lay its fabled bazaars, where merchants and artisans offered luxurious wares. Chinese caravans brought silks and fine porcelains, while cloth, gems, and spices came from Hindustan. There were local specialties like red velvet, prized everywhere, and Samarqand's paper, which Babur judged the finest in the world. Intricately woven carpets were offered; golden vessels and glass beautifully wrought.

Each trade had its own separate market, which Babur thought

SAMARQAND: MADRASA OF
ULUQ BEG, *photograph by Peter
Berger. Los Angeles County
Museum of Art.*
A *madrasa* is a traditional
Muslim religious college
where interpretation of the
Quran, religious law, and tradition are taught. The first
madrasahs developed in Central Asia, where Babur's
ancestors Amir Timur and his
son Uluq Beg built splendid
ones as a sign of their devotion
to Islam. This one stands on
the Registan, the main square
of Samarqand, and is covered
with beautiful tilework.

unique. He also noted the excellent kitchens and bakeries. Samarqand's food markets were piled high with round, fresh-baked flat
breads; baskets of precious rice, lamb, and mutton; and mountains of
local vegetables. Most tantalizing were the luscious fruits: crimson
peaches, fragrant melons, jewel-like pomegranates, and succulent
grapes.

The city was girded by massive walls so thick that one could gal-
lop a horse atop them. Surrounding these were numerous gardens
filled with fragrant blossoms, fountains, and pleasure pavilions.
"Few cities in the civilized world are as pleasant as Samarqand,"
Babur wrote. It was only natural that this young prince would lust
after the glittering metropolis. It was *the* center whose tastes set the
standard for the region's elite—and as Timur's capital, it possessed
immense prestige.

Samarqand was a worthy goal for an adventurous prince with

high ambitions. Yet, despite his many attempts to control it, the city continually eluded him. In the end, he finally abandoned it for another quest, Hindustan.

Babur attempted Samarqand's conquest four times in his life. The first was an unsuccessful siege laid in 1495, when he was only twelve and a half. On his second attempt, in 1497, he ruled the city for one hundred days but lost it when his forces deserted. At the same time, he was forced to rush back to Ferghana to recover his throne, which scheming nobles had handed over to his half-brother.

When he was forced to quit Samarqand the second time, the departing journey, sad enough, proved to be unlucky as well. Babur fell from his horse and onto his head. "Although I stood up immediately and got back on," he reported, "my brain did not return to normal until that evening. Events happening in the world were like dreams."

Throughout his journals there are similar terse descriptions of the wounds and illnesses that assailed him. There were far too many for such a youngster: sword wounds; arrows piercing his leg; deep, almost fatal fevers; and the effects of the cold and hunger that accompanied his rough existence. His utter stamina in the face of so much difficulty was amazing, no less than his great fortune amid the carnage of so many battles.

The next three years were not kind to Babur. He lost his throne, failed in his quest for Samarqand, was penniless, and was reduced to raiding small fortresses with a handful of followers. It was galling for a prince of his lineage and ambition. "It was difficult for me," he recalled years later. "I wept involuntarily."

In 1500 he geared up for another attempt on Samarqand. This time he stole the city from the Uzbek conqueror Shaybani Khan, but not for long. Babur held Samarqand for a little less than a year. The last few months were spent desperately besieged within the city. Babur was finally forced to accept a bitter truce with Shaybani Khan. Samarqand had to be surrendered, and Babur's own sister was given to the conqueror for a bride.

Babur had other, more personal, challenges in this period. In March of 1500, he celebrated his first marriage. The bride was his cousin, Ayisha Sultan Begum. The union was arranged by the two families, but Babur, then seventeen, did not easily take to it. "Although my affection for her was not lacking, since it was my first marriage and I was very bashful, I went to her only once every ten, fifteen or twenty days." Later on, still hopelessly bashful, he lost interest in his wife altogether. His irate mother took matters into her own hands. "Once every month or forty days my mother, the khanim, drove me to her with all the severity of a quartermaster," he recalled.

A Golden Opportunity

The year 1504 started off badly. Babur was fed up with Transoxiana and planned to go west to Khurasan, where he would hire himself out as a soldier of fortune. He had little wealth but set off anyway with three hundred poorly equipped followers. There was so little money that he only had two tents for his entire group, and one was reserved for his mother. His men had clubs instead of weapons, sheepskins instead of armor, and no horses. In this impoverished state, he received some advice en route to Khurasan that changed the course of his life.

A friendly nobleman, governor of a district, urged him to get as far away as possible from the dangerous Shaybani Khan and his Uzbeks. Better to head south, he told Babur, because in that direction lay a kingdom that was ripe for plucking. This was Kabul, capital of today's Afghanistan. Its ruler was an upstart, a non-Timurid, and weak to boot.

Fortune joined him as he seized this opportunity. His army had already begun growing as followers deserted other lords to join his camp. En route to Kabul he learned an excellent piece of news. Its king, warned of his approach, had already fled the city. Babur raced to occupy the vacant throne.

While riding through a mountain pass he glimpsed a good omen. It was dawn, and low on the horizon he saw a brilliant star ahead. Was it Canopus? he asked. It was. Canopus was a lucky star, highly auspicious, and Babur had never seen it before. Turning to him, one of his companions recited lines from a poem.

> Canopus, how far do you shine and when do you rise?
> You are a sign of fortune to all upon whom your eye lights.

Kabul

The good omen proved true. Practically without bloodshed Babur conquered Kabul by September 1504. It would be his for the rest of his life and a part of the Mughal Empire for more than two hundred years. After so much hardship he had finally gained a real kingdom for himself. He set about establishing a court that befitted a descendant of the great Amir Timur. Although it was small, he was quite happy with his new land.

Kabul was surrounded by mountains, a landscape that Babur favored. Its air was crystal clear and pleasant winds blew during the spring and summer. "No place in the world is known to have such a pleasing climate as Kabul," he stated happily. From the citadel there was a beautiful vista of a large lake and three meadows, which, when they turned green, were very pretty.

Surrounding Kabul were regions with varied climates, from semi-tropical to alpine. They sent many types of fruits and produce to the city's markets. Babur was impressed with the local wine, the grapes, plums, and citrus fruits. Abundant honey came from the surrounding mountains, and his transplanted fruit trees grew surprisingly well. Yet he also noted that sown crops like wheat did not do well, nor were the local melons very tasty. He felt sure that with seeds brought down from Khurasan good melons could be grown as well.

During his twenty years in Kabul, Babur settled down as best he could. He loved adventure and lost none of his ambition. Still, it was time to begin a family and create heirs for the kingdom. Like most princes he had the privilege of marrying a number of times and was obliged to establish a harem, the part of the palace reserved for women and children. The harem was where all of the young princes and princesses were brought up.

In 1507 Humayun, Babur's first son and heir, was born. Others followed, including his son Askari in 1516 and his youngest boy Hindal in 1519. Finally, a young princess with the delightful name of Gulbadan, or "Rosebody," was born in 1522.

A Love of Nature

Babur loved hiking in the mountains, and one of Kabul's attractions was its bracing air and mountainous surroundings. When younger he had taken refuge in a mountain village called Dakhkat. In his diaries he reminisced, "While in Dakhkat I used often to go for walks in the surrounding mountains. Mostly I walked barefooted. My feet got so that mountains and stones made no difference."

Babur had a deep love of nature. Insatiably curious, he was fascinated by landscape and wildlife. Now, with relative stability in his life, he could explore the fascinating natural world of his new possession. Babur toured his kingdom and noted everything with his alert eyes and inquiring, detail-oriented mind. Little escaped him, for he had a tremendous capacity for observation, worthy of a seasoned naturalist.

His memoirs devoted pages and pages to the region of Kabul. Listen to a description of the district of Nijrao, northeast of Kabul:

In the Nijrao Mountains are flying foxes, animals a bit larger than squirrels, with membranes between their arms and legs, like a bat's

PAGE FROM THE *BABURNAMA* SECTION ON HINDUSTAN: BIRDS IN A TREE, *ca. 1590. Courtesy the Board of Trustees, Victoria and Albert Museum, London.*
Throughout his memoirs Babur carefully described the animals and plants that he encountered. Here is an illustration from Akbar's Persian translation of the original manuscript, the *Baburnama,* describing the birds of Hindustan, one of the many depictions of the newly conquered land's wildlife.

wing. . . . It is said that these animals can fly from tree to tree as far as an arrow shot. I myself did not see one fly, but one was put on a tree, and it scrambled right up. Then they goaded it, and it spread its wings and sailed down as easily as flying.

Tied to his love of nature was his other great passion in life: making gardens. While he ruled in Kabul, Babur constructed no less than ten gardens, but his favorite was the Bagh-i-Wafa, which he built in 1508 on a rise overlooking a river.

The Bagh-i-Wafa, the "Garden of Fidelity," followed Persian design. It was a *charbagh*, or four-part garden. It was planned on a grid and had four subdivided squares planted with colorful blossoms and lush fruit trees. Dividing them were stone walkways and channels of flowing water. An ornamental pool lay in the center from which a fountain splashed water. With its views of the mountains, fragrance, and sound of running water, Babur's creation was a peaceful haven from the outside world.

Toward Hindustan

Despite the pleasures of life in Kabul, there were major problems. The most pressing was Shaybani Khan. He had conquered so much of the former Timurid lands that Babur was the only reigning Timurid prince left. The Uzbek intended to have more, and his forces advanced to the city of Herat, dangerously close to Kabul.

Another problem was that Kabul, although delightful, was poor. The kingdom was small and netted a very small income for its ruler. Babur had to find ways to increase his wealth. Without it he could not pay his followers, support his women and children, provide for the religious institutions, or support his court artists.

Despite his precarious situation, Babur now chose to change his title from *Mirza*, or Prince, to *Padshah*. It was a Persian title that had been held by his father, one signifying the highest rank, which claimed for him the legitimate leadership of all the remaining

Timurid nobility. His imperial Mughal descendants would adopt this title as well.

A title did not grant power, though, and Babur and his nobles were extremely nervous. It was only a matter of time before Shaybani Khan attempted the conquest of Kabul itself. To stay put would have been suicidal, for, as Babur pointed out, "there was neither any possibility for coming to terms nor any scope for resisting." Where to go? Some argued for flight to Badakshan, south of Transoxiana, while others suggested Hindustan.

This was not the first time Babur had thought of Hindustan. Long ago in the mountainous village of Dakhkat, where he had hiked in 1501, he had met a very old woman. Babur claimed that she was one hundred eleven years old, and she remembered tales that her cousin, a soldier with Amir Timur, had told to her. In 1398 he had been with Timur's forces when they invaded Hindustan. They had hauled back fabulous wealth, beyond anyone's wildest dreams.

In his diaries he confessed that ever since gaining Kabul, "I had craved Hindustan." Now, eager to explore the land he might have to flee to, he planned a campaign, but it was called off. By 1510 the Uzbek threat had diminished, and Shaybani Khan was dead. He had finally tangled with a ruler more powerful than he, the Persian emperor Shah Ismail, founder of the Safavid dynasty.

Shah Ismail opened diplomatic relations with Babur, and sent his sister, Shaybani Khan's wife, back to him. Then he dangled a tantalizing offer—Samarqand. In 1511 Babur had one last go at Samarqand, backed by the forces of mighty Shah Ismail. Like his earlier attempts, this one failed. He was caught between the demands of the Persians and the expectations of Samarqand's populace. He eventually lost support from both his backers and subjects and held the city for less than six months.

The final loss of Samarqand ended his sixteen-year-long quest for the city. In truth it was a lost cause. The land of Timur was now occupied by the Uzbeks, and they were there to stay. Babur had to make a choice. Should he stay in Kabul and accept his fate in a second-rate

THE MUGHAL GARDEN

Gardens had always been an important part of Muslim culture. From as far west as Spain's Alhambra to the eastern pleasure gardens of Timur's Samarqand, the planting and cultivation of gardens was an honored activity throughout the Muslim world.

The Muslim religion was born in the arid Arabian Peninsula. There, water and greenery signified life itself. Paradise, the reward of the faithful after death, was thought to be a garden. Within the Garden of Paradise, all was eternally green, and shade trees cooled the air. Fountains gushed water and cool springs flowed. Fruit trees filled with dates and pomegranates offered refreshment. There would be no end of sensuous delights.

Babur grew up in the garden tradition of Persian culture. For the Persians, the Muslim conception of the Paradise Garden coincided neatly with their ancient pre-Muslim beliefs. Persia, like Central Asia, knew extremes of climate throughout the year. Winters could be very cold, and summers were parched, but spring was a miracle of life renewed. For one brief period everything blossomed and the Iranian plateau was carpeted with masses of flowers. The last to bloom were the roses, the most beloved flowers of all, celebrated by Persia's poets. One of them, Hafiz, writing of springtime said: "Earth rivals the Immortal Garden during the rose and lily's reign."

The design of the Persian garden was based on straight, geometric lines. These axes were often walkways and water channels. Precious water was the key to their gardens. It was made to flow through long, straight channels, gush out of octagonal fountains, or rest in broad flat pools. In that part of the world, there were few babbling brooks, cool forests, or verdant lawns. Our "English"-style gardens with their natural, curving contours, massing of trees, and lush plantings would have been out of place.

The people of Babur's world were used to wonderfully intricate geometric designs in the tiles of their mosques, their carpets, and their holy books. The geometry of their gardens gave order and pleasure to their lives. Within the garden, the world existed in miniature. There was precious water to look at and its delicate sounds to bring delight. Cool shade from cypresses and evergreens brought a respite from the harsh sunlight, while lush floral plantings gave color and fragrance.

Later on, when the Mughals became established in Hindustan, this tradition of outdoor living influenced the design of their palaces, which have been called "tents frozen in stone." Babur was the first to establish gardens there on the Central Asian–Persian model. They were distant cousins to his earlier creations in Kabul, like the Bagh-i-Wafa, the "Garden of Fidelity."

درختهای انارهم هست کردا کرد د حوض تمام سه برگذار

جای من باغ همین است در وقت زردشدن نارنجهای بسیار

BABUR SUPERVISING THE LAYOUT OF THE GARDEN OF FIDELITY, *ca. 1590, painted by Bishndas, portraits by Nanha. Courtesy the Board of Trustees, Victoria and Albert Museum, London.* Here Babur oversees the building of his favorite garden in Kabul, the Bagh-i-Wafa, or "Garden of Fidelity." The man in front of him holds a board with a grid, a *tarah*, which contains the plan for the garden, from which all Persian-derived gardens were designed. The garden's squared-off planting beds contained varieties of flowers especially beloved by Babur.

kingdom or press on for something greater? He chose the second option; there was little in his character that would settle for the first. His quest was aimed in a new direction, south toward Hindustan.

Conquering Hindustan

In the space of seven years, from 1519 to 1526, Babur brought his army to Hindustan five times. The fifth and last time resulted in a great victory that laid the country at his feet. To win this new land Babur had first to challenge and defeat the Sultan of Delhi, Ibrahim Lodi. The sultan had an immense army and a vast treasury.

In the scorching month of April 1526, Babur estimated the opposing army at one hundred thousand men backed by almost a thousand battle elephants. His own forces numbered twelve thousand, but that included merchants and servants as well. Babur's men were nervous. They were not only vastly outnumbered but fighting in a strange land, where everything, including the language, was foreign.

Yet Babur had some important advantages over Ibrahim Lodi. One was his use of firearms, a new technology practically unknown in central Hindustan. These firearms, known as matchlocks, were a type of long gun that originated in Europe. The Ottoman Turks, whose empire straddled Europe and Asia, had started using these new weapons to great advantage. They had scored brilliant successes in battles with their eastern neighbors, the Persians.

When Shah Ismail of Persia started buying matchlocks to catch up with the Turks, Babur began arming himself as well. His forces used their time in Kabul to become expert with these weapons. In addition Babur brought a master Turkish gunner, Ustad (or Master) 'Ali-Quli, to supervise his artillery.

Babur's second advantage was his skill in battle. From an early age, he had been trained in the art of war. He was a seasoned tactician and could draw from his vast experience in the field. His fighters were not mercenaries, like many of Ibrahim Lodi's forces, but clansmen bound by codes of loyalty—if well treated. The promise of Hindustan's vast wealth was, no doubt, a powerful incentive for them as well.

Ibrahim Lodi knew but one kind of warfare, massive charges of soldiers and elephants. Babur's army was far more nimble. They were masters of horseback warfare and had both flexibility and advanced weapons.

The two armies met on April 30, 1526, upon the flat terrain of Panipat, north of Delhi. Babur prepared his lines days before. The town was at his back, and in front Ustad 'Ali-Quli had been instructed to harness carts together to form a huge defensive wall. This was known as the Anatolian method, after the Ottoman Turks who used it. Seven hundred carts were tied in a line with ropes, and space was left six to seven shields wide between them. Babur's gunners would stand and fire from behind the carts while the infantry was arrayed in front. Space was left every so often for the cavalry to charge in groups of 150.

For seven days in the mounting heat of April, the two forces faced off with no major action. One night the men in Babur's camp heard war cries. "The noise caused trepidation among those who had never witnessed such pandemonium," he recalled, "but the confusion was only a false alarm."

The next morning at dawn, Babur's scouts reported the sultan's immense forces advancing toward them. In a great cloud of dust and noise, Sultan Ibrahim's massed elephants and soldiers charged forward toward Babur's left flank. When they caught sight of Babur's forces, though, they seemed to hesitate, breaking the charge.

Babur sent his extreme left and right flank by prearranged plan around the sultan's forces to harass them from behind. Speeding forward on swift horses, they soon had the enemy forces almost surrounded. The sultan's men were shot at with arrows from the back and sides and pounded by massed artillery from the front. Try as they might to attack, they kept being pushed toward the center. Elephants trying to charge ahead were hit by arrows, and soon the sultan's forces could neither move forward nor carefully retreat.

By noon it was all over. Babur had won the day, and Ibrahim Lodi had perished. Babur reported that five or six thousand dead lay near the sultan's body, with the total number killed much higher. His men began gathering the surviving enemy soldiers and their commanders. Large numbers of elephants were rounded up and presented by the elephant keepers. This was something entirely novel, for Babur had never before possessed an elephant.

Babur was elated by his victory and proceeded on to Delhi to energetically tour its sights. He retraced the footsteps of his ancestor Amir Timur, who had conquered Delhi in 1398. One night, finally exhausted, he piled onto a boat on the river, got tipsy, and spent the night there. That Friday he had the *khutba*, the proclamation of his rule, read in the main mosque. The next day he sent his army to Agra and slowly followed, surveying his new terrain.

Meanwhile, Babur's son Humayun raced to capture the treasury at Agra, the capital, 124 miles away. While there he secured not only the treasury but a bit more. A wealthy Hindu ruling clan visiting Agra was preparing to flee after news of the defeat. Humayun's soldiers captured them, and, in return for a fortune of jewels, Humayun let them go. Among his sparkling loot was a famous diamond, the Koh-i-Nur, meaning "mountain of light," a huge stone whose value was said to equal what the whole world spent on food for half of a day.

Babur arrived in Agra and took possession of Sultan Ibrahim's capital. He gave thanks for his extraordinary victory and settled in. When Humayun excitedly presented him with the fabulous diamond, Babur simply looked it over and then handed it back to him. One day that gem would help Humayun repay a great debt.

Babur's Time in Hindustan

In the next few years, Babur settled into Hindustan, but the road was not entirely smooth. His troops were disenchanted with the country and wanted to return home to Kabul, loot in hand. Babur desperately needed them to maintain control in the newly conquered land. He called all of his men together and delivered a rousing speech that encouraged, even challenged them to stay. Many did, but others were only too happy to leave the heat, dust, and violent winds of their new conquest.

One departing commander scrawled poetic grafitti on the walls of his quarters. It said, in effect, that if he ever wanted to return to Hindustan may he be cursed forever. Babur was not amused. He quickly composed some verses and sent them off in reply. His response suggested that anyone who fled a rich empire because he didn't like the heat deserved to freeze.

Next Buwa, Ibrahim Lodi's mother, attempted to poison him. She almost succeeded, but Babur, becoming sick to his stomach, grew suspicious. He fed some of his food to a dog, which promptly grew sick as well. They both recovered, but an investigation was launched and the perpetrators punished. Shortly after that incident, a new and extremely serious obstacle arose, the military challenge of the Rajputs.

These valiant Hindu warriors were renowned for their military prowess. They had finally united under Rana Sanga, the king of Chitor, and had planned to confront Ibrahim Lodi's forces. Now that he was dead, they decided to challenge his conqueror, Babur. This was not just a war against intruders, but a struggle of Hindu leaders to reclaim territory lost centuries before. The prospect of fighting the Rajputs terrified Babur's men. These superb fighters had the reputation of being impervious to danger.

Babur needed to come up with a strategy. He had to rouse not only his men but the other Muslims of his new kingdom. He appealed to his fellow Muslims' fear of a Hindu resurgence by proclaiming this conflict a *jihad*, or holy war. To show his religious zeal, he followed an old custom and vowed not to shave until all of the infidels were defeated.

Finally, Babur made the dramatic gesture of giving up alcohol.

**BABUR'S ARMY CAPTURING
THE FORT AT CHANDERI IN
1528,** *ca. 1590, painting by
Kibman Sangtarash, outline by
Makand. Courtesy the Board of
Trustees, Victoria and Albert
Museum, London.*
After Babur's decisive defeat
of Rana Sanga's Rajput con-
federation in 1527, there were
still other Rajput chieftains left
who challenged his power.
One of them was the ruler of
Chanderi, to the south of
Agra, who was an important
ally of Rana Sanga. Babur
won Chanderi in 1528 and
was impressed with the architecture of the conquered fort.

Prior to that, in defiance of Islam's prohibition on drinking alcohol, Babur had drunk to excess. Many eastern Muslims did as well, but now, genuinely repentant, he gave it up. Others followed his example and their smashed golden wine goblets were distributed to the poor. Another rousing speech was made to encourage his men, and they all swore oaths of loyalty to Babur on their holy Qurans.

The battle took place at Khanua, west of Agra, on March 17, 1527. The Rajputs put up a much better fight than the forces of Babur, but in the end they were defeated. In a grisly custom dating from Mongol times, masses of their severed heads were piled into towers by Babur's soldiers. Now that he was the undisputed master of central Hindustan, Babur added another name to his title, *Ghazi*, "holy warrior for Islam."

A Strange Land

Babur could finally relax. He was in Hindustan to stay and dispatched his older sons to take up the governorships of its various provinces. The ladies and children of Babur's harem were conveyed from Kabul to Agra to take up residence there. In these final years, Babur worked on his memoirs, assembling his jottings over the years and dictating his recollections. As in Kabul, he made pages and pages of notes about Hindustan, its people, customs, landscape, and wildlife. He described a bird native to the country:

> Parrots are of many varieties. One is the sort that is taken to our country and taught to talk. . . . Another sort is smaller . . . and it too can be taught to talk. This sort is called the "jungle parrot," and there are many of them in . . . that region. When they fly in flocks of five or six thousand, a difference in the size of the bodies of these two variations is evident, although their color is the same.

He followed with another parrot:

BABUR DICTATING HIS
MEMOIRS, *ca. 1610. Raza
Library, Rampur.*
Toward the end of his life,
when he had finally conquered
Hindustan, Babur set about
organizing his diaries and
memoirs. Here he dictates to
a scribe, who writes down the
emperor's story. To Babur's
right, two young court pages
hold a fly whisk and Babur's
swords.

The red one is nicely shaped. It can be taught to talk, but unfortunately its voice is as unpleasant and shrill as a piece of broken china dragged across a brass tray.

In truth he didn't really like Hindustan. It was too strange, too different from his beloved Kabul and Ferghana. He found its climate horribly oppressive. The landscape of Central Hindustan was "flat as boards," and its cities, for one used to splendid Samarqand, "unpleasant." He had a lot of criticisms for the new land:

> Hindustan is a place of little charm. There is no beauty in its people, no graceful social intercourse, no poetic talent or understanding, no etiquette, nobility, or manliness. The arts and crafts have no harmony or symmetry. There are no good horses, meat, grapes, melons, or other fruit.

On the other hand there were some things that he liked. "One nice aspect of Hindustan is that it is a large country with lots of gold and money."

Babur determined to bring some of the familiar things that he craved to this strange and wealthy new environment. Water, for one. There was nothing in Hindustan like the waterways that irrigated Transoxiana's fields and gardens. "I always thought one of the chief faults of Hindustan was that there was no running water," he said. "Everywhere that was habitable it should be possible to construct waterwheels, create running water, and make planned geometric spaces."

Those "planned geometric spaces" were his beloved gardens. He was disgusted at first by Agra's disorderly terrain but finally founded two gardens on the north banks of its Yamuna River. One was called the Gul Afshan ("flower scatterer") and the other the Zar Afshan ("gold scatterer"). In each he built a garden complex with ornamental pools, courtyards, a house for bathing, and plots for roses and narcissus. "Thus," he boasted, "in unpleasant and inharmonious Hindustan, marvelously regular and geometric gardens were introduced." For Babur these gardens were not just a labor of love, but a highly symbolic statement of power. By building them Babur brought the glorious royal tradition of Amir Timur and Samarqand to his new land.

Even today it is said that an abandoned garden on the banks of Agra's Yamuna was built by Babur. It is called the Arambagh but is thought to be his Gul Afshan garden. If so, then that is where Babur was first buried. On December 21, 1530, only four short years after he won Hindustan, Babur died. He wanted to be laid to rest in Kabul, and finally, during his son Humayun's reign, he was. In accordance with orthodox Muslim law and his own simple wishes, he asked that his tomb be open to the sky.

Today, in the tragic, strife-torn city of Kabul, Babur's tomb still stands. His imperial descendants embellished the grave site with a mosque and fine marble railing. They looked on him with reverence, and admired his qualities of courage, intelligence, and fairness. They studied his military strategy. They adopted his love of nature as well, creating great gardens and superb depictions of animals and flowers. And they were proud that through Babur their ancestry came from the legendary Amir Timur. One hundred sixteen years after his death, Shah Jahan, Babur's great-great-grandson, tried to recapture Samarqand. He was an avid reader of the *Baburnama,* and longed to make good on his ancestor's four-time quest. He didn't, but Babur still inspired his vision.

Babur established his dynasty in Hindustan as surely as he planted his gardens. Toward the end of his memoirs, Babur described returning home to Agra from an expedition. His gardener, Balkhi, had harvested the first melons planted in his absence and had kept some for him to taste. "They were very nice little melons," he recalled. He was pleased with the ways things were working out. "I was particularly happy that melons and grapes could turn out so well in Hindustan." His dynasty would turn out brilliantly.

Chapter 4

NASIR UD-DIN MUHAMMAD HUMAYUN

What Happened to Din-panah?

One hundred miles south of Panipat, where Babur won Hindustan, lies the sprawling city of New Delhi, India's modern capital. New Delhi was built by the Colonial British in the early part of this century to be the capital of their Indian empire. It was named New Delhi to distinguish it from the adjacent and ancient city of Delhi. Within the combined borders of the two cities—now united—lie the sites of at least eleven earlier cities. Delhi's earliest city still lives on in the legends of the ancient Hindu epic *Mahabharata*. It was called Indraprastha, the capital of the mythic Pandava brothers. Recorded history dates the first city at Delhi within one hundred years before the birth of Jesus, but others surely preceded it.

Since then, many rulers chose to build their capitals there. They erected grand structures, thrived for a time, and then perished. Today those ambitious capitals survive as ruins only, surrounded by the modern metropolis.

One of those kings was Babur's son, Nasir ud-Din Muhammad Humayun, who inherited the throne in 1530. When he became

EMPEROR HUMAYUN, *early-nineteenth-century copy of a Mughal painting. Metropolitan Museum of Art, New York.*

emperor, Humayun decided to build a new capital for his reign. His father had settled in Ibrahim Lodi's former capital at Agra, but Humayun chose to build elsewhere. His city would be built at Delhi, the ancient site of kings and sultans. It would be the new dynasty's first great building project, and Humayun was excited. He had carefully chosen its name, *Din-panah*, the "Asylum of the Faith."

An asylum is a place of safety, a haven for those in danger. Humayun had inherited his family's appreciation of culture and learning. In his day, religious thinkers and philosophers were persecuted in Persia, Turkey, and other parts of the Muslim world. "Asylum of the Faith" was intended as a place of refuge, where they could live and work free from persecution. If Humayun could attract these highly educated people to his court, then Din-panah might soon become a leading cultural center like lost Samarqand.

The court historian Khondamir, whose *Humayun-nama* chronicled the early years of Humayun's reign, told the story of Din-panah's foundation. In the flowery, elaborate Persian used for Mughal court chronicles, he described the scene:

> In the middle of the month of the sacred Muharram 940 (1533), at an hour which was prescribed by the most clever astrologers and the greatest astronomers, all of the great *mushaykhs* [religious leaders] . . . the learned persons, and all of the elders of the city of Delhi, accompanied the king, who was as generous as the ocean, to the spot, prayed the Almighty God to finish the happy foundation of that city, and to strengthen the basis of the King's wealth.

First, "His Majesty with his holy hand put a brick on the earth," then each person from the distinguished assembly followed. The crush of the crowd prevented the workmen from even approaching the site that day. Nevertheless the walls and gates rose quickly. According to Khondamir they were almost finished within ten months.

Today, over four hundred and fifty years later, the site of Din-panah still exists, although largely ruined. It is now called *Purana*

Qila, the "Old Fort," and it sits atop a long, grassy ridge in New Delhi. Much of what is left was built by Sher Shah, who conquered Din-panah from Humayun and built his own city there. Despite that, some memories of Humayun still remain. Even as a ruin the Purana Qila is impressive. Thick round battlements swell out from the fortress's high stone walls. The ramparts shelter lofty stone gates crowned with domed pavillions called *chattris*, and they are pierced with deep, pointed archways. One gate facing south is called the Humayani Darwaza, the Gate of Humayun. It stands almost intact.

A Letter to Humayun

On November 28, 1528, Babur sent a letter to Humayun, then twenty years old. The prince was posted to Badakshan, a distant province northeast of Kabul. Prince Humayun Mirza, like his brothers, Kamran Mirza and Askari Mirza, had been sent to far-off provinces to rule in their father's name. Babur wrote to his sons in order to learn news of their districts, and to give advice.

His letter to Humayun began warmly: "Thinking of you with much longing, I greet you." He then congratulated him on the birth of his son, named al-Aman. Babur gently voiced concern that the newborn's name might be a bit too unusual. He also feared that the common people would mispronounce it. "Nonetheless, may God bless and keep both him and his name."

He had other concerns, as well. Humayun was not the energetic leader Babur had hoped for, judging by the advice he gave:

> Do not fail to make the most of an opportunity that presents itself. Indolence and luxury do not suit kingship. Conquest tolerates not inaction; the world is his who hastens most. When one is master one may rest from everything—except being king.

This anxious father's letter shows us a young prince who is slightly aloof, not aggressive enough, and perhaps a bit too fond of luxury. Humayun's style was very different from his father's. As emperor, he saw himself continuing the great Timurid tradition of luxury and patronage on a lavish scale. His father had done the hard work of getting the dynasty to Hindustan. Now Humayun would establish its splendor.

If Humayun had looked closely, he would have seen that the time was not yet right for lavish display. There were other, more pressing concerns. His dynasty, for instance, was far from secure.

Astrological Administration

In the first years of his reign Emperor Humayun began putting into practice his administrative philosophy. While it was rooted in time-honored concepts of how to structure society, it did not turn out to be particularly practical. Despite his noble aims, Humayun was hardly the effective ruler that the young dynasty needed.

He was extremely dependent on astrology, a system of prediction based on the position of the stars and planets. In Hindustani culture astrology was, and remains, an extremely important system for ordering people's lives. In Humayun's day royal courts throughout Hindustan, and many parts of Europe and Asia, maintained resident astrologers. They were routinely asked to offer the best dates for battles, royal marriages, or even the beginning of young princes' studies. Even today, many modern Indians will consult astrologers before planning important life events.

In Humayun's world, omens, both good and bad, were seen as guides for the future. Babur himself rejoiced when he saw the lucky star Canopus, an omen of good things to come. Yet father and son diverged in their dependence on these things. Babur maintained a healthy skepticism. One example is his reaction to an astrologer at the time of his battle with Rajputs at Khanua:

Muhammad Sharif, the doom-and-gloom astrologer, although he did not dare speak to me personally, . . . told everyone he met that Mars was presently in the West and anyone who fought from that direction would suffer defeat.

His predictions didn't discourage Babur, who won a smashing victory. Immediately after the battle, the astrologer rushed in to congratulate him. Babur paid him for his past services and ordered him to leave the country.

There is a well-known story told by Khondamir about Humayun when he was still a prince posted to Badakshan. One day while riding with some companions, he announced that he wished to take an omen from the next three people he would meet on the path. He would ask their names. Based on their meanings he would know his future.

The first person he encountered was a forty-year-old man. His name was Murad, meaning "pleasure." The second, driving a donkey loaded with wood, was named Daulat, meaning "government" or "the state." At this point Humayun confided in his companions that if the third was named Sa'adat, meaning "good," then his future would be assured. Just then a young boy came by leading his cattle. His name was Sa'adat, and Humayun was elated.

The story is not only charming, but also highly symbolic. Daulat, Sa'adat, and Murad corresponded to the ways that Persian Islamic tradition saw the divisions of society. According to Khondamir, Humayun set about dividing his courtiers and the upper ranks of society into three classes, based on these divisions.

The first group was called Ahl-i Daulat, "officers of the state." This included his family, the nobles, ministers, and the military. The second was the Ahl-i Sa'adat, the "good men." This included religious figures, teachers, philosophers, thinkers, poets, lawgivers, and everyone else who was highly respected. Finally there were the Ahl-i Murad, the "people of pleasure." These were the young people who possessed beauty, who were elegant, and musicians, whose talent gave pleasure.

Next, the schedule of government was reorganized around these classifications. Each group was allotted two of the week's seven days. On those days the imperial court concerned itself only with issues relating to that group. Humayun choose the specific days according to astrological guidelines. In that system each day was ruled by a specific planet, so he tried to link the symbolism of the planet to his three classes. In addition he wore a different color, based on the planet, for each day of the week.

Saturdays and Thursdays, for example, were allotted to the "good men." Saturday was ruled by Saturn, protector of religious and respectable men, while Thursday was under the sign of Jupiter, protector of the learned. The learned, the pious, and the poetic visited the court on these days. Khondamir himself, with his flowery language, would have come to court then: "On these two days the tree of hope of this estimable body of the people produced the fruit of prosperity by their obtaining audiences in the paradise-resembling Court."

Sundays and Tuesdays were for the "officers of the state," and for government business. These were also the days when Humayun mounted an especially opulent display of power for his subjects. Like all absolute rulers, he knew that he needed to create a strong and splendid impression on his people. When Humayun appeared before the people, the deep thudding of great drums announced that he was about to appear, while the loud roar of guns heralded his departure. Later he gave audience to his nobles, distributing valuable robes of honor and gifts of money to those he wished to reward.

On Tuesdays he administered justice. Criminals were brought in, while executioners, swords in hand, stood before his throne ready to carry out their punishment. Mondays and Wednesdays, on the other hand, were devoted to pleasure. Friday, the holy day of assembly in the mosques, was when all of the groups gathered together at court.

Humayun divided the government into four departments. Each

was based on one of the four elements: Earth, Fire, Water, and Air. Earth took care of agriculture and buildings. Fire controlled arms production and the military. Water was responsible for waterworks and canals, while Air got stuck with the imperial kitchen and the stables.

During this time Humayun indulged his love of pleasure. He constructed a fabulous floating pleasure pavilion on the Yamuna River, beneath Din-panah's walls. There, lit by hundreds of torches, and perfumed with incense, he listened to music with companions, sipped wine, and took opium. For pleasure as well as amusement, he had a huge round carpet made that was painted with astrological symbols. In the center, standing above the image of the sun, stood the emperor. His courtiers stood around him and rolled dice with images of different activities. Whichever image faced up they had to enact.

Under Humayun's style of administration, the dynasty's grip on Hindustan began to loosen. His troubles began to mount, but not all of them were his fault—especially at the beginning. Babur had begun the dynasty with significant victories, but the Mughals only controlled a small central part of the country, and powerful enemies remained. In reality the dynasty was a shaky upstart in a complex, ancient land.

It needed a focused, dynamic leader to steer it through its growing pains. Humayun was not that man.

The Troubles Begin

There were three critical challenges to Humayun's early reign. The first was the growing power of regional leaders on the periphery of his territory. The second was his brothers' ambitions. Each had been given a portion of Mughal lands to rule upon their father's death, and naturally they wanted more. The third challenge was perhaps his deepest problem . . . himself.

Humayun's approach to administration was clearly neither practical nor realistic. Babur had cautioned him not to isolate himself. He sensed that his son needed the balance of other opinions to have a better grasp of reality. Whether he recognized his son's growing opium addiction as well is not known.

The emperor was now in his early twenties and had a mounting fondness for opium taken with wine. This led to long periods of indolence and indecision, crippling for the head of a young dynasty. Just when he needed to be bold and aggressive, he would pause for months, retiring to the pleasures of the harem. He possessed skill and courage as a military leader but had poor judgment.

His most dangerous enemy by far was Sher Khan Sur. Like Ibrahim Lodi, Sher Khan was an Afghan nobleman whose family had lived in Hindustan for generations. Hindustan's Afghans bitterly resented the Mughals for defeating the Lodi dynasty. They were anxious to restore Afghani leadership to the realm.

Sher Khan was both smart and extremely capable. His family's lands were in Bihar, a province east of central Hindustan. His first move was to capture neighboring Bengal, the wealthy easternmost province. With its money and resources, he could rapidly build up a powerful force to challenge the Mughals. In 1537 he invaded Bengal and besieged its capital at Gaur.

Humayun recognized the threat of Sher Khan's growing power but took so long to reach Bengal that Sher Khan had long departed. There was still time to catch up with him and strike a blow at his forces. But Humayun dawdled. Even Jauhar, his faithful, admiring servant, couldn't understand it. "He very unaccountably shut himself up in his harem," Jauhar wrote later in a book about the emperor, "and abandoned himself to every kind of indolence and luxury."

The Troubles Get Worse

Sher Khan was now confident enough to openly challenge the Mughal forces. They met in March 1539 at Chausa, halfway down the Ganges. Both armies settled in on the same side of the river, which flowed directly behind Humayun's camp. For three months they dug in and improved their defenses. They both possessed heavy artillery and, like Babur at Panipat, each set up a long wall of artillery carts from which they could pound the other side.

Envoys shuttled back and forth with negotiations. Finally, a settlement was reached. Sher Khan would be awarded two provinces but only by acknowledging Humayun as his overlord. Humayun was pleased with the outcome and ignored a friendly warning to be on his guard. Jauhar, recalling that night thirty years later, wrote:

> The King would not believe the information, or that Sher Khan would be guilty of such a breach of honor and religion, and passed the night without taking any precautions.

Just before sunrise an incredible uproar was heard at the rear of Humayun's forces. It was Sher Khan's army staging a surprise attack. Lulled into a false sense of security, Humayun had advanced beyond his defensive position, exposing his forces. Suddenly everything was in chaos. The Afghans charged wildly into the sleeping camp, slaughtering everyone in sight. Humayun desperately tried to mount a cavalry charge, but to no avail. Masses of troops, troop followers, and even members of the harem ran screaming for the river, pursued by the rampaging Afghans.

One of Humayun's nobles seized the bridle of his horse and shouted that he must flee before it was too late. The emperor rode hard to the river, followed by his war elephants, but when he entered the Ganges his horse sank from beneath him. All around him people were drowning as they tried to escape. Those remaining on land were being massacred by the Afghans. Only by a miracle was

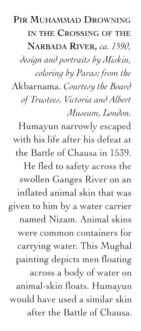

PIR MUHAMMAD DROWNING IN THE CROSSING OF THE NARBADA RIVER, *ca. 1590, design and portraits by Miskin, coloring by Paras; from the* Akbarnama. *Courtesy the Board of Trustees, Victoria and Albert Museum, London.* Humayun narrowly escaped with his life after his defeat at the Battle of Chausa in 1539. He fled to safety across the swollen Ganges River on an inflated animal skin that was given to him by a water carrier named Nizam. Animal skins were common containers for carrying water. This Mughal painting depicts men floating across a body of water on animal-skin floats. Humayun would have used a similar skin after the Battle of Chausa.

Humayun's life saved. A water carrier inflated the animal-skin bag that he used for carrying water. With this float the emperor made it to safety across the river. There—with screams coming from the other side, with the bloodied bodies and drowned horses floating by—he turned to the water carrier and asked his name. It was Nizam. Humayun promised Nizam that he would sit on his very throne as his reward.

Exile

Chausa was the beginning of the end. Vast numbers of Humayun's forces perished. Those ladies of the harem who hadn't drowned were captured, including the empress Haji Begum. Sher Khan had won a great victory, so great that after his victory he proclaimed himself ruler of Hindustan. He took the title Sher Shah.

Humayun made it back to Agra, where he finally consulted with his brothers. At this time Nizam the water carrier showed up in Agra, eager to claim his reward. To his brothers' disgust Humayun fulfilled his promise. While his empire lay in shambles, Nizam was seated upon the throne and allowed to play king for two hours.

Less than one year later, in May of 1540, a demoralized Mughal army faced Sher Shah's forces at Kanauj, one hundred miles from Agra. The battle ended in utter defeat for the Mughals, their forces slaughtered by the Afghans. Humayun fled across the Ganges once again, this time on an elephant. Somehow he reached Agra, grabbed what he could, and fled for the northern city of Lahore. Sher Shah followed, leisurely occupying all of Humayun's former realm. He took over Din-panah in 1540. There he formally proclaimed the Sur dynasty, based on his family name.

For the next fifteen years, Humayun was exiled from his empire in Hindustan. The first four years were spent wandering back and forth with his dwindling forces. Perhaps the only positive note in this whole period was his marriage to Hamida Begum, a young noblewoman.

As the hot season set in, their wanderings through the desert became unbearable. There was little water, few horses, and bad feelings besides. One of the low points came when the pregnant Hamida did not have a horse for a day. The soldiers refused to help her, so Humayun dismounted and gave her his own horse. There was nothing left for him to ride except a camel, a very undignified mount for a former emperor.

One more happy event occurred in the midst of their troubles. Hamida gave birth to a son, Akbar, in the desert village of Umarkot in 1542. By 1544 Humayun seemed trapped. His brothers Kamran and Askari actively conspired against him, while Sher Shah was eager to see him dead. He attempted to flee to Qandahar, a border fortress near Persia, but that route proved impossible. Askari controlled Qandahar and wanted nothing more than to seize Humayun for Kamran. Finally, the only alternative left was to attempt an escape to Persia and throw himself on the mercy of its ruler, Shah Tahmasp.

It was the month of December. Now, instead of scorching deserts, Humayun's route would wind through high, frozen mountains and snow-covered passes. This was a hard journey in the best of times; the terrain was treacherous and the route notorious for the thieves who preyed on its caravans. There was another danger as well. His fourteen-month-old infant Akbar would almost certainly not survive the terrible journey. Something had to be done to preserve the child's life.

Humayun appealed to his family's deepest code of honor. Like the medieval knights of Europe, the descendants of Amir Timur held certain values sacred. One of them was that their children and women were to be protected. Despite Askari's open enmity, Humayun knew that his child would be safe with him. Hamida wept as she placed her baby in the care of their faithful servant Jauhar. The former emperor steeled himself against the thought that he might never see his son again. With heavy hearts they rode out to their uncertain future.

While Jauhar delivered their son into the safekeeping of Askari's wife, Humayun and Hamida made their way to Persia. They had only a few loyal soldiers and hardly any servants. Food was scarce. Their first night they had to boil horse's meat in a soldier's helmet. Sitting in the snows of the mountain pass, chewing on boiled horse's meat, Humayun must have grieved for everything he had lost and feared for the future. What if the shah turned him away? Where could he go then?

EARLY MUGHAL PAINTING

When the art-loving Humayun visited the court of Persian Shah Tahmasp at Tabriz, he met two painters from the court studios, Mir Sayyid Ali and Abd as-Samad. These two masterful artists eventually followed Humayun to Kabul, where they taught drawing to his son Akbar, and then on to Hindustan. After Humayun died they directed Akbar's court studios and helped found the new Mughal painting style. Many of the painters at Akbar's court were Hindus, and the new style combined both Persian and Hindustani elements. The Persian masters' style was full of intricate, realistic details, elegantly rendered in jewel-like colors. Hindustani art, by contrast, was much less realistic, using bold designs and vivid colors.

Unlike the large canvases that we associate with Western painting, most of the paintings in the Persian and Hindustani tradition were small, often designed to illustrate books. They were more like the illuminated manuscripts of the Middle Ages. This type of painting is called miniature.

The adventure-filled Hamzanama *was one of Akbar's favorite books and told the magical tales of the legendary Hamza. It was one of the first major projects of Akbar's studios. The vigorous composition, filled with intricate details, is typical of the new style that emerged from Akbar's studios.*

Persia and Beyond

Humayun's fears were realistic. Kamran had already tried to make a deal with Shah Tahmasp, but the shah's influential sister urged her brother to receive Humayun warmly. When his group straggled into Persia from their tortuous journey, they were greeted as visiting roy-

EARLY MUGHAL PAINTING

PERSIAN PAINTING:
LIFE IN THE CAMP
*ca. 1540, by Mir Sayyid Ali.
Harvard University Art Museums,
Arthur M. Sackler Museum,
Cambridge.*

HINDUSTANI PAINTING:
AKRURA PRESENTING THE
JEWEL SHYMANTAKA TO
KRISHNA, *ca. 1520–40, Mewar
School. Courtesy the Board of
Trustees, Victoria and Albert
Museum, London.*

MUGHAL PAINTING: GARDENERS BEATING GIANT ZAMURRUD TRAPPED IN A WELL, *from the* Hamzanama, *ca. 1562–67, supervised by Mir Sayyid Ali and Abd as-Samad. Courtesy the Board of Trustees, Victoria and Albert Museum, London.*

SHI'ISM

There are two major religious groups within the Muslim world, the Shias and the Sunnis. Most Muslims are Sunnis, but a significant minority belong to the Shia sect, which is centered in Iran, part of the former Persian empire.

The two groups differ in a number of ways, but most important is their conflicting claims to legitimate spiritual descent from the Prophet Muhammad. These conflicts were similar to Protestant Europe's challenges to the Catholic pope's authority based on his spiritual descent from the apostles of Jesus. Leadership conflicts arose within the Muslim world less than one hundred years after the death of the prophet. Muhammad's first four successors were known as the caliphs, and although the first caliph was part of Muhammad's family, the rest were not. Muhammad's son Ali challenged the caliphs' authority and was killed. Afterward, his son Husain took up his father's cause and was martyred at Kerbela, now in Iraq, in 680 C.E. Husain's followers were known as Shias.

Ever since, the Shias have looked on Husain as a revered figure. In the Muslim month of Muharram, they mark his death with passionate ceremonies of mourning. These recall the similarly intense sorrow of Catholic Good Friday ceremonies in Spain and Italy.

alty. Servants saw to their every need, rich clothes were provided, palaces were put at their disposal, and exquisite meals were offered.

Humayun toured the country and visited the marvels of Persian culture, which his ancestors had so appreciated. He saw beautiful mosques covered over with brilliant tiles, exquisite gardens with graceful pleasure pavilions, and sumptuous palaces.

Humayun was properly impressed with everything that he saw. He was particularly attracted to the jewel-like paintings produced by the imperial court's studios. There he met the leading painters, among them Mir Sayyid Ali and Abd as-Samad. Humayun had no throne, much less an imperial court to invite them to, but he extended an invitation to them anyway.

That they accepted two years later showed the desperate changes they had been through. Shah Tahmasp was an increasingly devout member of the minority Shia sect, which predominated in Persia. As he became increasingly orthodox, the shah abandoned his generous patronage of painting. Painted imagery of figures were traditionally forbidden in the Muslim faith, but the Persians had long maintained a distinguished artistic tradition. Shortly after Humayun left Persia, the shah closed down the imperial painting studios. The two painters Humayun liked best now needed his patronage.

Since the zealous shah was rich and powerful, he could easily support Humayun in his bid for reconquest. What better opportunity for his sect than to send Humayun back to Hindustan at the head of a Shia dynasty? While the prospect of lavish military support was dangled before him, strong pressure was applied for Humayun to convert. It was a package deal, so to speak; without conversion there would be no support.

Humayun wavered, but ultimately he had little choice. If he didn't accept, the alternative was too grim to contemplate. He finally accepted conversion. The shah was elated and threw a magnificent feast to celebrate. Humayun was sent off with money, arms, and a force of twelve thousand Persian soldiers.

Before he left Persia, Humayun wanted to repay the shah for his lavish year of hospitality and for his military support. Through his five years of anxious wanderings, he had carried with him a small pouch of jewels, treasure taken from Agra. He left some jewels as a thank-you gift for the shah. Some speculate that among them was the fabulous Koh-i-Nur diamond. Then he set off.

Reconquest

Within seven months, on September 3, 1545, Humayun took Qandahar. Two months later Kabul fell and Kamran fled before his brother's powerful forces. At Kabul, Humayun and Hamida were joyfully reunited with their son Akbar, now three years old.

For the next eight years, Kabul went back and forth between Kamran and Humayun, but finally Humayun won it. For the first time in his life, his brothers no longer posed a threat to his power. Loyal Hindal died battling for him, and both Askari and Kamran were imprisoned and sent off on a pilgrimage to Mecca, where they too died.

Regaining Hindustan

While Humayun wandered miserably about the desert, Sher Shah set up an effective administration at his new capital. He renamed the city *Shergarh*, meaning "Fort of Sher Shah," and built new buildings there. During his brief reign he instituted economic reforms, and set about reorganizing the system of landholding. So effective was this system that Akbar, Humayun's son, used it as a model during his reign. Sher Shah also built many roads, improving communications in his vast realm. One of them, the Grand Trunk Road, still exists today, running north from Delhi toward the Punjab.

Five years after he founded his dynasty, Sher Shah died. He was succeeded by his son Islam Shah, who died nine years later in 1554. Hindustan quickly descended into chaos as three nobles fought for control of the throne. There was no leadership, cities were plundered by competing troops, and petty rebellions broke out. The way was clear for Humayun to retake Hindustan. This time his judgment was sound, and he was aided by his superb general, Bairam Khan, a loyal follower.

On July 23, 1555, Humayun regained the throne and the remains of Din-panah. Bairam Khan was awarded the position of commander-in-chief, with the title Khan-i Khanan, the "lord of lords." Liberal rewards were distributed to his followers, and even Jauhar, his loyal servant, was appointed to the minor nobility.

The old city was now filled with various new buildings, among them a fine mosque built by Sher Shah. Yet, at least one building of Humayun's remained, a tall, graceful octagonal structure with a domed pavilion on top. Today that building is known as the Sher Mandal. Until recently it was thought to date from Sher Shah's time, but its decoration is more likely a product of Humayun's early reign.

The Sher Mandal was probably used as Humayun's library. Books and art were two of his greatest interests, and in Mughal times they were inseparable. Paintings were made primarily, though not exclusively, for books. Humayun particularly enjoyed spending time under the domed pavilion of the Sher Mandal's roof, and would sometimes conduct business there. On January 24, 1556, he sat there giving audience to a group of pilgrims recently returned from Mecca. It was the late afternoon and must have been extremely pleasant. At that time of year, Delhi enjoys crisp, clear days, and late afternoons are often bathed in golden sunlight.

The meeting was over and Humayun prepared to descend the steps. On the second step he heard the call to prayer from Sher Shah's nearby mosque. He turned to bow reverently toward Mecca, but as he got up his foot caught in his robe. He tripped down the steep steps and fell head first against them. For three days he lingered, barely conscious, and then he died.

His councillors were terrified. What would become of the reestablished dynasty? Akbar, the heir to the throne, was hundreds of miles away doing battle under Bairam Khan's supervision. They hid the news of the emperor's death and hastily improvised. A cleric was found who bore a slight resemblance to the emperor. They dressed him up in the imperial robes and stood him high upon the walls for the twice-weekly public appearance. The populace, standing far below, cheered the man they thought was their ruler. This charade continued for seventeen days.

Messengers were rapidly dispatched to the loyal Bairam Khan. Humayun wisely had appointed him regent in case of his own death. Akbar, then only thirteen, was crowned in the middle of a field. He was just a bit older than his grandfather, Babur, had been when he was made king. Like his grandfather, Akbar would have the ambition and dynamic vision needed to forge a powerful empire.

Humayun's Tomb

If you stand atop the Sher Mandal's roof facing south, you will see a majestic domed structure in the distance. With its impressive, swelling white marble dome, it almost resembles the Taj Mahal. Closer inspection reveals the differences, but here, nevertheless, is one of India's most distinguished buildings. It is Humayun's tomb, the first major edifice erected by the restored dynasty. It was built by

HUMAYUN'S TOMB, *old postcard*. This photo, taken in the early part of the century, shows Humayun's regal tomb sitting amid its spacious garden in what is now New Delhi. Its closest architectural relative is another imperial tomb, the Taj Mahal, built later at Agra, 124 miles to the south.

Humayun's senior widow, Haji Begum. Akbar sponsored the monument, a tribute to his father, and a powerful symbol of his own rule.

Today the tomb stands in a large area scattered with old buildings. As you approach you pass by an old domed mosque set in a small walled garden. Then a shady avenue of banyan trees leads you to the entrance gateway. Once you enter you have left the city far behind. Before you lies a huge Persian garden whose broad lawns surround Humayun's final resting place. In Akbar's time these gardens held fruit trees and colorful blossoms. Water sprayed from fountains and coursed through marble channels, but now, sadly, they are all dry. Still, the tomb remains impressive. It sits upon a spacious platform, and its earthy reddish color is dotted with white marble highlights. From the top of its dome a thin finial swirls skyward, covered with gold.

The building's style was something entirely new. It is Mughal, harmoniously blending the dynasty's diverse roots. The helmet-shaped dome comes from Samarqand. In place of Central Asia's azure tiles, it is covered in native white Indian marble. The facade echoes Persia, but faced with Delhi's distinctive reddish-pink sandstone. The roof is crowned with small domed pavilions called *chattris*, an inheritance from the architecture of the 300-year-old sultanate of Delhi. Finally, the spacious gardens recall Persia and Central Asia. They reflect Babur's first efforts to bring his beloved traditions to the foreign land.

In building Humayun's tomb, Akbar announced that this young dynasty was finally home and there to stay. It was a tribute, as well, to his father, the emperor who just barely made it all possible.

Chapter 5

ABU'L FATH
JALAL UD-DIN
MUHAMMAD AKBAR

A Great Ruler

Akbar was the greatest ruler of the Mughal dynasty. He can only be compared to the other great monarch whose lifetime coincided with his own, Queen Elizabeth I of England. His reign was dynamic and animated by his superhuman energy. He was larger than life and excelled at almost everything, from making war to appreciating art.

Akbar has been called India's great philosopher-king. He balanced his abundance of worldly gifts with a deep, thoughtful, inquiring mind. Earnestly he sought answers to his spiritual questions, and despite the intolerance of his era, he grew to respect all religious traditions.

Singlehandedly, with courage, wisdom, and determination, Akbar made the Mughals what they ultimately became. He created their glory and bound it to Hindustan's fate. If Akbar was responsible for building all of this, then what forces were responsible for creating him? How did such greatness emerge from a tiny infant left behind by fleeing parents?

Like Akbar himself, his story has many parts. Abu'l Fazl, his best

AKBAR ENTERTAINED BY AZIM KHAN, HIS FOSTER BROTHER AND FAVORITE AT DIPATPUT, *outline by Jagan, painting by Surdas. Courtesy the Board of Trustees, Victoria and Albert Museum, London.*

friend, counselor, and court chronicler, wrote down his version of the emperor's life. His chronicle filled three volumes and was called the *Akbarnama*. Within its pages lie Akbar's great adventures. They led him to the heights of worldly glory, but sometimes to deep understanding as well. An imperial hunt was the setting for one tale.

Incident at the Qamargah of 1578

Dust and noise swirled upward in the frantic stampede of terrified animals. Stags, gazelles, and antelopes called *nilgai* raced madly for a safety they couldn't reach. There was no escape. They were penned in a huge circular enclosure whose only exit was death.

In one long, deadly leap, a sleek, spotted cheetah felled a stag, teeth buried in its throat. Whoosh! An arrow pierced a running nilgai. It stumbled, fell, and was trampled by the frenzied animals. A turbaned man chased in hot pursuit, his magnificent steed gaining on a wild-eyed gazelle. Raising his sword high he swung and cut deeply into the panicked gazelle's side.

This was the *qamargah*, the Mughal hunt inherited from their Mongol ancestors. Like the great hunts enjoyed by European royalty at just this time, the imperial Mughal hunt was both sporting event and awesome display of power. Thousands of troops were drafted for the emperor's hunts. Squadrons of beaters surrounded vast areas of the countryside. Steadily they drove the wildlife toward a large round, fenced enclosure, the qamargah. At its center stood the imperial tents, temporary palaces for the emperor's hunting party.

Once the animals were penned within the qamargah, the first few days belonged to the emperor. Akbar was an avid hunter, as keen for the chase as for going to battle. His imperial cheetahs assisted the hunt. These swift, leopard-like natural hunters had been trained by the Mughals to snare their prey. Cheetahs, like the nobility, were graded and ranked. Their greatest hunters wore jeweled collars and

AKBAR STAGES A HUNT NEAR LAHORE, *ca. 1590, outline and portraits by Miskin, painting by Sarwan, from the* Akbarnama. *Courtesy the Board of Trustees, Victoria and Albert Museum, London.* Here is all of the energy and excitement of an imperial hunt: Akbar gallops with sword upraised, ready to strike at the fleeing animals. In the painting's upper right-hand corner and lower part, the fenced *qamargah* (Mughal hunt) enclosure is depicted. At bottom center there is an imperial cheetah bringing down its prey; at center the women of the harem within the imperial tent and the eunuch guardian sitting outside; and at bottom right an elephant whose driver carries an elephant prod in his right hand.

ate the choicest meats. The hunt was ranked as well. When the emperor had finished, the high nobles went in, then the lesser, and downward to the common soldiers. Hunting was a respected tradition that was not only an amusement, but a way of training the troops for battle. No one felt badly about the slaughter.

This particular qamargah was held in 1578, in the Punjab village of Bhera. Akbar was thirty-six years old and in full command of his powers. His reign was in its twenty-third year, and he had long since proved worthy of his name, which means "the Great."

Since the time of his father, the empire had tripled in size and wealth. Magnificent cities had been built, a powerful army created, and new, effective reforms promoted. Three hundred wives filled the imperial harem, and beyond that, a priceless treasure as well: three male heirs. Akbar possessed everything the world could possibly offer, but he was not happy. From time to time a sadness descended upon him and his splendid life felt empty. He searched for deeper meaning and prayed for an answer.

Consider what happened at the qamargah. The orgy of killing was reaching its peak, and the heap of slaughtered animals mounted ever higher. Abu'l Fazl the court chronicler described what happened next: "All at once a strange state and strong frenzy came upon the emperor, and an extraordinary change was manifested in his manner, to such an extent as can not be accounted for."

At that very moment Akbar stopped the hunt, overcome with grief over the senseless slaughter. The nobles were stunned, and silence descended. Struggling to master his strong feelings, the emperor communicated to those nearest him that the animals must be set free.

At that moment Akbar was feeling more than just grief. His body was trembling. His eyes had filled with a strange light and a smile of wonder spread across his face. A powerful force was shaking him to the roots of his being. This was a moment of religious revelation: "A sublime joy took possession of his bodily frame." A spirit of awe had entered Akbar. In that moment Akbar saw that he and the hunted animals shared in the same life spirit. How could he destroy these innocent beings?

For days Akbar remained in an ecstatic state. He was grateful for his experience and expressed his thanks as a devout Muslim would. He prayed and generously distributed money to holy men and the poor. He even filled a large tank at his palace clear to the top with coins for charity. Then, honoring his own strong feelings and Hindu tradition, he prohibited the killing of animals, for a time. Finally, he vowed to stop hunting.

The Prince's First Lessons

From early on Akbar had a mind of his own, and he wasn't concerned about breaking the rules. He would rather play sports than learn from books. Akbar adored anything physical, whether it was wrestling, hunting, flying pigeons, or playing polo.

The last was a real passion. Polo is a ball game played by teams on horseback. It requires expert command of one's mount, swiftness, and dexterity. Akbar never lost his devotion to the game, which increased as he aged. Later in life he invented a glow-in-the-dark ball from a special type of smoldering wood. With this invention he managed to play polo even at night.

Akbar's devotion to sports was not unusual in young boys. What was unusual was that Akbar never properly learned to read. Many think that he was able to read somewhat but did so only with great difficulty. Some speculate that he might have suffered from a type of dyslexia, a learning disability in which text appears backward to the reader. In any case, young Akbar could not, or would not, read, which shocked his cultivated family. Perhaps they had forgotten that their most illustrious ancestor, Timur, was also illiterate. Despite this handicap he triumphed brilliantly over his problem. His son, Jahangir, left this description from his memoirs, the *Tuzuk-i Jahangiri:*

GAME OF POLO, *ca. 1650, from the* Large Clive Album. *Courtesy the Board of Trustees, Victoria and Albert Museum, London.* This painting illustrates one of the Mughals' great sporting passions: polo. The game originated in Central Asia and required expert command of one's mount, a skill acquired in battle training.

Although he was illiterate so much became clear to him through constant intercourse with the learned and wise, in his conversations with them, that no one knew him to be illiterate, and he was so acquainted with the niceties of verse and prose compositions that his deficiency was not thought of.

By his twentieth year, Akbar began employing a staff of special readers. Great works of literature, history, and philosophy were read to him almost every day. He personally marked the place where they had finished for the day and rewarded them with gold and silver coins according to the number of pages read. With his formidable intelligence and the knowledge from his readers, Akbar became highly informed. He also developed an extraordinary memory. He slept little, remembered everything, worked ferociously, and kept everyone on their toes. The empire reaped the benefits.

Akbar's Feats

As he grew older, Akbar's feats of daring became legendary. He was completely fearless and thrived on physical danger. He encountered tigers in the countryside and slew them singlehandedly. He charged into battle at the head of his forces, impervious to bullets, swords, and arrows. His greatest feats, however, were when he mounted mast elephants and brought them under his control. The mast gland is present in male and female elephants and becomes active under stress or in mating season. When male elephants go into a period of mast, they grow extremely aggressive and dangerous. They will throw or kill their drivers, charge people, and attack other elephants.

Elephants were the Mughals' imperial beasts, and only the emperor could stage fights between them. Like the ancient Romans, the Mughals were addicted to animal fights, but elephants never fought to the death. Imperial Mughal palace complexes usually had a large field called a *maydan* where these entertainments were held. The elephant fights were arranged once a week before the imperial residence at Agra.

When Akbar was nineteen, he decided to arrange a match between two formidable elephants, Hawa'i and Ran Bagh. Hawa'i, which means "sky rocket," was so renowned for his ferocity that elephant drivers were reluctant to mount him. Now that he was in mast, they were terrified even to approach him.

Akbar decided that he would mount Hawa'i for the fight. His chief minister, Atgah Khan, implored the young emperor to stop before it was too late, but Akbar typically ignored his pleas. The two elephants fought wildly, trumpeting and crashing their tusks against each other. When Hawa'i finally triumphed over Ran Bagh, the defeated elephant suddenly panicked, turned, and ran. The enraged Hawa'i raced after him all the way to the river with Akbar holding on. Both elephants ran onto a pontoon bridge that spanned the Yamuna River, and the bridge promptly began to bob and heave as if it was going to sink. Somehow the bridge held long enough for Akbar to subdue his ferocious mount. As Hawa'i calmed down, Ran Bagh escaped to the other side with his life and tusks intact.

Adham Khan's Fall

While Akbar's physical feats promoted his almost superhuman image, the empire couldn't run on physical courage alone. A ruler had to claim the absolute power that was his by right and then fight to maintain it throughout his reign. When Akbar was a teenager, he stood poised at a critical moment in his reign. There were powerful people blocking Akbar's path. His goal was to clear these people away so that he alone could steer the empire. The first obstacle was Bairam Khan, the regent. Although he was Akbar's friend and mentor, he had begun to misuse his power. In 1560, when Akbar turned seventeen, he was persuaded to dismiss Bairam Khan. The general was "invited" to go to Mecca, a form of banishment, but he was showered with gifts and honors as befitted a loyal friend of the dynasty. On his way out of Hindustan, Bairam Khan was murdered.

Akbar's next challenge was the two unscrupulous people who had plotted Bairam Khan's downfall, Maham Anga and her youngest son, Adham Khan. Maham Anga was a highly ambitious noblewoman who had been one of Akbar's wet-nurses, a privileged position that reaped benefits for both her and her son. The greatest benefit was close contact with the young emperor. Adham Khan soon revealed his unsavory character, a mixture of dishonesty, cruelty, and a vicious temper.

In May of 1562 Adham Khan showed who he really was. Akbar

AKBAR'S HISTORIAN

Akbar commissioned a large number of books to be written and illustrated at his court, among them works of history. Historical writing was important to the Muslim world, an interest partly inherited from the Greeks, Romans, and Persians. Akbar employed scholars who compiled histories of Hindustan, the Muslim world, and his ancestors, among others. He saw the great value of creating dynastic histories, a way to record a dynasty's achievements while advertising its importance throughout the literate Muslim world.

The historian most linked with Akbar's court was Abu'l Fazl, who was not only a scholar, military commander, and diplomat, but a close friend of Akbar's as well. In 1587 he started work on his monumental three-volume history of Akbar's reign. It was called the Akbarnama, the "Book of Akbar," and it was illustrated by the court's leading painters. Abu'l Fazl also completed another monumental work called the A'in-i Akbari, which was something of an almanac or encyclopedia on Akbar's reign. Within its pages there was information on everything from crop yields per district to recipes on how to make kulfi, a Mughal form of ice cream.

Because Abu'l Fazl was both court historian and friend of the emperor, his work was extremely flattering to Akbar. Most Mughal emperors had chronicles of their reigns compiled, and without exception these records told the official version only. Unflattering details were either left out or removed by the emperors.

The occasional exceptions were found only in secret histories that were left unpublished during their author's lifetimes. One of the best of these was the Muntakhab al-Tawarikh, written by Abd ud-Karim Kadir Badauni, a scholar at Akbar's court. Badauni knew Abu'l Fazl from childhood but strongly disagreed with him about Akbar's religious policies. His history, like Abu'l Fazl's, told the story of Akbar's reign but from a different, less flattering point of view. Comparing these two works is one most interesting way to study Mughal history.

had appointed a new chief minister, Atgah Khan, the man who had begged him not to ride the mast elephant Hawa'i. Maham Anga and her son bitterly resented his appointment. They correctly saw that it was the beginning of their fall from power. One day, six months into his job, the new chief minister was meeting with other courtiers in the palace, dealing with affairs of state. Akbar was in rooms nearby within the harem, taking a nap.

Suddenly, "Adham Khan came violently in with a party of ruffians more violent than himself." According to Abu'l Fazl, Adham Khan walked up to Atgah Khan, hand on his dagger, and eyes glaring with rage. Everyone stood still for one brief moment. Adham Khan nodded to one of his henchmen, who plunged his dagger into Atgah Khan's chest.

The bleeding minister ran in terror toward the emperor's nearby rooms. Before he could reach them, the assassins slashed him to death in the courtyard. The courtiers screamed loudly as Adham Khan ran toward Akbar's rooms in the harem. He jumped up on the outer balcony and attempted to force his way into the harem, but a guard had barred the entranceway. Akbar was awakened by all of the commotion and a servant relayed the alarming news.

He rushed out to see Atgah Khan's bloodstained body lying on the courtyard pavement. Someone handed him a sword and he rushed off to find the murderer on the balcony. Cursing him loudly he demanded to know what had happened. Adham Khan grabbed the emperor's hands and pleaded with him not to judge without investigation, but Akbar threw his hands off and tried to grab his sword. When Adham Khan resisted Akbar punched him, and knocked him unconscious.

Now the murderer's fate was sealed. The guards were ordered to bind him, lift him off the balcony, and throw him to his death. He fell onto a hard stone floor, but was not killed, so his broken body was hauled up again. Once more he was thrown, and this time "his neck was broken and his brains knocked out." With no regrets, but concerned for Maham Anga, Akbar went to her quarters and gently broke the news. Forty days after, she died, her power broken.

**AKBAR ORDERS THE PUNISH-
MENT OF HIS FOSTER
BROTHER ADHAM KHAN,**
*ca. 1590, design and portraits by
Miskin, coloring by Shankar, from
the Akbarnama. Courtesy the
Board of Trustees, Victoria and
Albert Museum, London.*
This dramatic painting depicts
Adham Khan falling to his
death. After killing Akbar's
chief minister, Atgah Khan
(who lies dead at bottom left),
Adham Khan approached
Akbar (upper left). The young
emperor punched him unconscious and then ordered him
thrown to his death from the
balcony.

She and her son were buried together at Delhi, and Akbar erected a monument over their tomb. It stands to this day, a domed octagonal building on a high platform near the first Muslim tower in Delhi, the Qutb Minar. Atgah Khan lies buried in Delhi as well. His monument lies not far from the gardens of Humayun's tomb. Akbar had seen the dire results of letting others gain influence over him. From that point on he ran the empire by himself.

Peace and War with the Rajputs

Akbar had the right instincts for building a strong empire. He knew that he needed a superb army, an effective administration, and as much land as he could conquer. He built up an immense fighting force and kept them occupied at all times. He once said:

> A monarch should be ever intent on conquest, otherwise his neighbors rise in arms against him. The army should be exercised in warfare, lest from want of training they become self-indulgent.

With the military operating full time, Akbar could threaten his neighbors with invasion. Sometimes he merely went hunting in their vicinity. With thirty thousand troops in attendance, they quickly got the message. For Akbar's neighbors there were only two options: alliance and incorporation within the Mughal Empire, or war.

Yet the young ruler possessed a broad vision of how the empire could function. He believed that former enemies could become strong allies if they were well treated. In a letter to his son Murad, he gave advice about the art of ruling:

> Let not difference of religion interfere with policy, and be not violent in inflicting retribution. Adorn the confidential council with men who know their work. If apologies be made, accept them.

In a country like Hindustan, people had long memories and vengeance remained a threat for generations. Akbar saw that flexibility and accommodation would ultimately serve the empire well. He balanced his powerful war machine with careful diplomacy, and soon enough many enemies became staunch allies. He offered them their lands and power in return for their support.

Among the greatest challenges to Akbar's expansionist goals were the fierce Rajput kingdoms. Akbar needed them to secure the heartland of his empire. Without them his western flank would always be exposed to an internal enemy. With them by his side, the empire could expand to the limits of the subcontinent. If he wasn't going to conquer them, then he would need alliances with them. The question was, were they willing to be at peace?

Appealing to the Majority

Akbar pursued relations with the Rajput rulers for two reasons: his grasp of the political situation in Hindustan, and his ideals. When he looked at the three-hundred-year-old history of Muslim Hindustan, he perceived a major problem. None of the dynasties had lasted very long. Even the history of Delhi was proof of this, for by Akbar's time six different capitals had risen and fallen there. The Muslims' problem was that their power base was too fragile.

The Muslim dynasties were a thin upper crust ruling a huge Hindu populace. Discriminatory practices were designed to make Hindus feel inferior to Muslims. Consequently many Hindus felt little loyalty to their Muslim rulers. Without their support, no one could really hold on to the country for very long.

In comparison with the treatment of Jews or Muslims in Christian Europe, discrimination by Muslims in Hindustan was relatively mild. It had to be, since the Hindus were an overwhelming majority. On the whole, Muslims and Hindus lived peaceful but separate lives. Nevertheless, there were deep problems that have remained to this day. Akbar had the vision to address those problems directly. Through his genius Hindustan's Hindu populace

was offered a place in his realm, a first in three hundred years of
Muslim rule.

Akbar viewed the Rajputs as the most glorious nobility of his vast
Hindu population. From the beginning, the young emperor keenly
desired to be emperor of all his people, not just his fellow Muslims.
Because Akbar did not grow up in Hindustan, he was freer of preju-
dices than most Hindustani Muslim rulers. He only arrived there
with his father's reconquest, when he was almost thirteen. Hindustan's foreign ways, its peoples, and exotic wildlife must have
strongly appealed to him. He became fascinated by the Hindu religion and interested in its customs. Like Babur he was bright and
deeply curious. Unlike him, he quickly felt at home in his new land.

In 1562 he added a new wife to his harem, a Rajput princess. She
was the daughter of the raja of Amber, head of a minor clan whose
kingdom lay due west of Delhi. While Hindu women had joined the
harems of earlier Muslim dynasties, they were never allowed to keep
their religion. Akbar's new wife was allowed to worship freely. From
that moment on, all Hindus within the harem were free to follow
their own faith.

It was the custom to give princesses honorary names upon their
marriages. The princess of Amber was given an exalted title,
Maryam az-Zamani, which means "Mary of the Age." This referred
to Mary, the mother of Jesus, whom Muslims revered. The marriage
accomplished many things. It brought Rajput prestige as well as military and administrative skills to the Mughal court. Within a few
years, it also brought them an heir to the throne. By the time of
Akbar's grandson, Shah Jahan, all of the imperial princes were
partly descended from royal Rajput families.

The Rajputs soon formed the basis of a new Hindu aristocracy at
court. Alliance with the rapidly growing dynasty assured these
rulers wealth and increased power within their own realms. They
were allowed to keep their titles and lands in return for allegiance to
the emperor and military support for his dynasty.

The newly enriched Rajput courts began modeling themselves on

> *To distinguish between them, Muslim and Hindu noblemen at the Mughal court wore their* jamas, *or robes (the source of our pajamas), buttoned on different sides. Muslims wore their* jamas *buttoned to the right, while Hindus wore theirs buttoned to the left.*

the imperial Mughals, with royal audiences, formal etiquette, court painters, and sporting events. Rajput members of the aristocracy soon rose to distinguished positions within the realm. Raja Man Singh of Amber, for example, who served as a leading general and later as governor of the province of Bengal, became a member of Akbar's inner circle.

Akbar's openness to the Rajputs extended downward through the Hindu population. The civil service was opened up to Hindus, who flocked to fill many positions. Soon Hindu artists and musicians joined the court as well. One of Akbar's prize cultural achievements was luring the legendary Hindu musician Tansen to his court. Among his most favored painters was Daswanth, a brilliant Hindu artist, who was said by Abu'l Fazl to have "surpassed all painters and become the first master of the age."

What really endeared the Hindu population to Akbar was his abolition of two discriminatory taxes. The first was a tax on pilgrims, paid when they visited their shrines. This was abolished in 1563. The second was a general tax called the *jizya*, which was levied on all non-Muslims within the kingdom. It was bitterly resented, and when he abolished it in 1564, Hindus were most grateful.

Despite the happy results of this new policy, there were some Rajput leaders who refused to join the Mughals. Udai Singh Sisodia, the maharana of Mewar, was one of them. Perched in his capital at Chittorgarh, he looked down on all of the Rajput leaders who had joined the emperor. The maharana was the Great King of Mewar, the premier lord of all the Rajput kings. While most Rajput rulers carried the title of *rana*, he alone was called *maha*, meaning "great" *rana*. His family was the most ancient and therefore most proud. He would have nothing to do with the young Mughal emperor. His pride and Akbar's ambition clashed in one of the greatest confrontations of the reign.

Chittorgarh

Chittorgarh was formidable. Its immense, rocky outcrop rose high and solid from the surrounding plains, as if Nature itself had planned the mighty fortress. From the top, almost six hundred feet up, a sheer precipice dropped to the land below. It was more than three miles long, over half a mile wide, and ringed by massive walls. For centuries it had been the proud capital of the kingdom of Mewar. Chittorgarh was the symbol of Rajasthan, seat of its most esteemed rulers.

The origins of the fort and its rulers lay in legend. Some said that the fort was originally built by Bhim, one of the five Pandava brothers from the Hindu epic *Mahabharata*. The ruling house traced its lineage as far back as 700 C.E., and it was said that they were descended from the sun itself, through great Rama, a form of the god Vishnu.

Before Akbar's time Chittorgarh had been conquered only twice. The first time was in 1303, when it was gained for the love of its beautiful queen, Padmini. The powerful sultan of Delhi, Ala ud-Din Khilji, had heard of her beauty and requested but one glimpse. It was forbidden to see or meet the queen, but Ala ud-Din was allowed to view her reflection in a garden pool. He was so smitten that he determined to possess her. He captured her husband, but the king was soon freed by his own men. Shortly after that, Ala ud-Din besieged the fort and, after an immense battle, conquered it. He controlled it for the next twenty-three years.

When the defenders realized that they were about to lose, their women and children performed the harrowing ritual of death by burning. While smoke rose from living funeral pyres, the warriors donned their saffron robes, the color of holiness. After swallowing opium, they opened the gates of their fortress. Charging forward, they shouted the names of their gods as they rode to certain death.

SIEGE OF RANTHAMBHOR
(left side) Akbarnama, c. 1590. Design by Miskin, coloring by Paras. Courtesy the Victoria and Albert Picture Library.
This depicts the siege of the fortress at Ranthambhor, a Rajput stronghold that was attacked by Akbar's forces one year after Chittorgarh fell. Here, in the left-hand scene of a double painting, teams of bullocks and men strain to pull cannons up the steep incline of the hill. At the top, Akbar's cannons are being fired at the enemy fortress, while his artillerymen crouch for protection behind leather shields.

When Ala ud-Din finally entered Chittorgarh's gates, there was no one left within. Padmini herself had perished in the flames as well.

After that it was conquered once more, by the sultan of Gujarat in 1535. According to historians of the time, thirty-two thousand Rajput soldiers perished in that battle and thirteen thousand women died in the flames. Now, just thirty-three years later, Chittorgarh was once again ready for a confrontation.

The fort was actually a small city, filled with stone temples and palaces. One was a 120-foot-high stone victory tower, built in 1440 to commemorate the ruling house's defeat of Muslim forces. Because the fort contained natural springs, there would be no lack of water in case of siege. The maharana stored enough food to supply the defenders for years. He also laid waste to the countryside so that Akbar's forces could not live off of the land.

Still, the maharana decided to leave before the battle. He knew that the fort could be taken. If his dynasty was to live on without joining the hated Mughals, he had to create a second city. Seventy miles away he created a new fortress in a valley ringed by tall hills that overlooked a large lake. That site, one of India's most beautiful cities today, was named Udaipur after him, and it became his new capital. Meanwhile the maharana left the fort with a garrison of eight thousand men. They were commanded by two young leaders named Jai Mal and Patta. The fortress could potentially hold out for years.

Akbar arrived at the base of the fort in October of 1567. His forces included both Muslims and Hindu Rajput allies. The immense Mughal camp spread for ten miles on the plains below the fort, a sight that no doubt intimidated its defenders.

Akbar had worked out his plan of attack. There were two major ways to get at the enemy above. The Mughal historical chronicle *Tabaqat-i Akbari* described the methods that Akbar used to gain the fortress:

> The emperor ordered the construction of *sabats*, and the digging of mines. About five thousand builders and carpenters and stonemasons were collected, and began their work of constructing *sabats* on two

MUGHAL MILITARY ENCAMPMENTS

Like the ancient Romans, the Mughals were masters of military organization. Akbar spent approximately one-fourth of every year in the field. When he went to battle, he took with him an immense, entirely mobile city of tents. A precise plan set out the place of everything, from the imperial tents to the streets for the bazaars. Each time the camp was moved, it was reassembled on the same plan, so that its inhabitants could always find their way around.

At the center of the camp stood the brilliantly colored, elaborate tents of the emperor, including a section reserved for the harem. Surrounding them were the tents of the high nobility, and in the next ring the lesser nobility. The city had its own mosques, hospitals, and bazaars, where merchants flocked to offer goods. The war elephants and cavalry horses were housed in mobile stables. When it was time to move on, the camp was broken down and placed onto the backs of camels and bullock carts. The camp traveled ahead of the emperor so that when he arrived at the next field site, the city lay ready for him.

sides of the fort. A *sabat* is a kind of wall which is begun at musket-shot distance (from the fort), and, under shelter of its planks strongly fastened together and covered with rawhides, a kind of way is conducted to the fortress. The walls are then battered from it with guns and a breach being made, the brave assailants rush into the fort.

Slowly and tortuously the *sabats* snaked their way up the hill, gaining Akbar's forces protected access to the massive walls above. They were so wide that ten horsemen could ride abreast on them, and high enough that an elephant with riders could pass under. Building them was a dangerous process, especially at the front ends.

AKBAR ATTACKING THE FORTRESS AT CHITTORGARH
Akbarnama, c. 1590. Design by Miskin, coloring by Bhura and Jarwan. Courtesy the Victoria and Albert Picture Library.

In this double painting's left-hand scene, the artists have captured one of the Siege of Chittorgarh's most dramatic moments. A mine accidentally exploded, killing hundreds of troops, both Akbar's forces and the fort's defenders. Akbar is depicted at the very bottom with his left arm outstretched. There are bodies of soldiers, and even a horse, propelled through the air from the explosion's terrific impact. At the top right, the buildings of the fort are depicted, including the tall, spire-like towers of its Hindu temples.

Sharpshooters from the fort above picked off the workers, whose only protection was leather screens set up as shields. Each day almost two hundred laborers were killed this way.

Tunneling explosives under the walls was also quite effective, but many of Akbar's most celebrated fighters perished at Chittorgarh in a terrible explosives accident. Sappers had climbed up the rock and dug strategic tunnels under the walls. Finally they had placed explosives under two key neighboring bastions. The plan was to explode both at the same time and create a huge breach. A large force of handpicked fighters stood ready to rush the walls immediately after they had been blown open.

WHAT DOES CHITTORGARH TELL US?

Today there are some who point to the slaughter at Chittorgarh as proof that Akbar was no friend of the Hindus. In the heated ground of today's Hindu/Muslim conflict in India, Mughal history has been re-examined. Even Akbar, a ruler celebrated for his tolerance, has been held up to new scrutiny.

The truth is that Akbar's siege of Chittorgarh was first and foremost a struggle for power, and not a religious war. The innocent victims were not killed for their Hindu religion, but to create an example that would intimidate future enemies. In slaying the fort's civilian inhabitants Akbar was broadcasting the brutal but effective message that he would crush any opposition to his empire. Hindus fought on Akbar's side in this battle, and at other times he did battle against Muslim forces. In the remaining thirty-seven years of his reign Akbar never again killed Hindu innocents on this scale, and his Hindu subjects grew to revere him.

The first bastion blew up with a huge roar. The troops rushed into the breach and prepared to enter the fort. The Rajputs charged forward, determined to repel them. What none of them knew was that the second fuse had taken longer to reach the explosives than expected. Disaster struck. According to the *Tabaqat-i Akbari:* "The second mine exploded and the bastion was blown up. Friends and foes, who were contending in the breach, were hurled into the air together, and those also on whom the stones fell perished."

The explosion was so terrific that huge stones were propelled great distances and bodies were found scattered in the plain. At least five hundred were killed by falling stones alone and countless others died in the actual explosion.

After this tragic setback Akbar renewed his determination to capture the fortress. By now the *sabats* had wound their way up the hill and come very close to the walls themselves. From a special platform atop one of the *sabats,* Akbar could actually see inside the walls. His forces massed for a nighttime assault through the gap made by the explosion. Jai Mal, the commander of the fort, stood in the breach encouraging his defenders. By his side were his mother and wife, valiantly defending the fort. According to some historians, Akbar was just able to see him in the light of the gunfire and rocket flares. He aimed his favorite gun, Sangram, and fired. Jai Mal was killed on the spot.

That immediately turned the tide. With their leader dead, the garrison's defenders knew that Chittorgarh would soon fall.

> The garrison was disheartened by the fall of their leader, and each man hurried to his own home. They collected their wives, children, property and effects in one place and burnt them.

The fighting went on all night, but by the morning the fortress fell. The defenders were all massacred by Akbar's orders. After that a far greater slaughter took place, again by the emperor's command. Chittorgarh housed approximately forty thousand Hindu civilians within the fort, mostly servants and peasants. Akbar ordered these innocent people to be slain as well. All day long his forces slaughtered people within the fort, even those who had fled to the sanctuary of the temples.

Akbar's victory was complete. Chittorgarh had been utterly devastated and its inhabitants crushed. It was the most critical victory of his early reign. After Chittorgarh there was one more major Rajput fortress to conquer, Ranthambhor, to the northeast. In 1569 it fell to the Mughals as well. There remained some minor engagements and the unconquered maharana in his new capital. Later emperors would deal with his descendants. For now Rajasthan had been subdued.

In its long history, Chittorgarh had risen three times from the ashes. It would never rise again. Today it lies as a shadow of its former self. Sections of the walls remain, as do some temples, ruined palaces, and the famous Tower of Victory. There are also some small villages, but for the rest, scrub, bare ground, and ghosts inhabit this once proud citadel.

Chapter 6

THE VISION OF
FATEHPUR SIKRI

In his well-protected realm, the borders of which extend to the great salty ocean, there was room for practitioners of various sects and beliefs, both true and imperfect, and strife and altercation were not allowed. Universal harmony was his rule, and he conversed with the good and pious of every sect, creed, and religion and attended all according to their condition and understanding.

This tribute is from the memoirs of Jahangir, Akbar's son, and it pays homage to one of his father's greatest achievements: promoting religious toleration. Viewed in the context of Akbar's time, it ranks as one of the most extraordinary features of his reign. While the emperor eased discrimination and invited sages of various faiths to his palace, neighboring Muslim countries actively persecuted members of their minority sects. Northern Europe convulsed with religious wars, while the Spanish Inquisition burned heretics at the stake. Even the distant New World witnessed extreme intolerance. Native peoples whose beliefs differed from their conquerors' were forcibly converted, enslaved, or killed.

Even now Akbar's reign remains a shining example of how diversity can be respected. Today's India—and much of the contemporary

AKBAR PRESIDING OVER DISCUSSIONS IN THE IBADATKHANA *(detail)*, *ca. 1605, by Nar Singh, from the* Akbarnama. *Chester Beatty Library, Dublin.*

117

world—still struggles with these issues. Akbar showed that tolerance can be promoted by an able ruler. He also proved that it can bring strength and glory to a land.

The Master Builder

Twenty-four miles from Agra, in the midst of barren countryside, a high, majestic gateway crowns a rocky ridge. On the ridge's long spine stand the remains of Akbar's extraordinary palace city, Fatehpur Sikri. This four-hundred-year-old ghost town now lies deserted, but parts are so well preserved that it seems as if Akbar's courtiers might stroll by at any moment.

Fatehpur Sikri was like no other place in Hindustan, and its architectural style drew on the shared heritage of its people. These elements had already blended through centuries of coexistence, but Akbar's architects brought them to a new level of refinement. His palace city was a living expression of his ideas on kingship, politics, art, and religion. Here he came into his full maturity as a ruler, father, and person.

Yet, only fourteen years after Fatehpur Sikri was built, it was abandoned as a capital, never to be used again. That symbolized Akbar as well. He was a ruler who couldn't stop moving. Wherever he happened to be was, for that moment, the center of the empire. Being on the move was deep in Akbar's blood, for he was descended from nomads. The memory of their crude Central Asian encampments lived on in his tented military cities and in the richly ornate tents that graced his gardens.

Despite his attachment to movement, Akbar was also in love with building. Building was the supreme art that married his personal tastes to his ambitious political ends. An historian at Akbar's court, Qandahari, put it this way: "A good name for kings is achieved by means of lofty buildings." By erecting beautiful and impressive buildings, Akbar would add prestige to his reign. At a time when there was no television or newspaper advertising, architecture was one of the most effective ways to broadcast the news of a dynasty's wealth and power. Just as Humayun built Din-panah as an emblem of his dynasty, so Akbar now rapidly embarked on an ambitious building program.

His first major venture was the Red Fort at Agra, on the banks of the Yamuna River. Akbar had moved his capital from Delhi back to Agra and had taken over the old Lodi dynasty brick fortress there. He was intent on creating something far better. In 1565 he began the reconstruction of the fort. It took eight years to build, and when completed it was one of the wonders of his age. More than five hundred buildings stood within its massive red sandstone walls. The walls rose more than seventy feet high, with blocks so well joined that, according to Abu'l Fazl, "the end of a hair would not find a place between them." Flanking the main gateway were two huge carved stone elephants, each with larger-than-life riders. These were a tribute to his slain enemies, Jai Mal and Patta, who commanded the Chittorgarh fort.

It was an awesome sight and conveyed a clear message about Mughal power. William Finch, an English traveler, described the fort at length in his journals of 1608–1611. He was quite taken with it, remarking that it was "one of the fairest and admirablest buildings of the East." Akbar's walls still stand, as impressive as ever, but only one of his five hundred buildings remains. His beloved grandson Shah Jahan tore the rest down to make way for his own exquisite structures.

While he was completing both Agra's fort and his father's tomb in Delhi, Akbar began another large-scale project, Fatehpur Sikri. Why did he need another capital so close to Agra? And what compelled him to select that rocky, unpromising site for a major palace? The answer lay with his fervent desire for an heir and with a holy man who lived high on the ridge at Sikri.

The Prophecy of the Shaykh

Fortune smiled on Akbar. Everything he touched turned to gold, and whatever he desired was his. Everything, that is, except for a son. Without a son all of his hard work might go to waste. Dynasties needed heirs to survive, but despite his growing harem, Akbar had not yet produced a son. Male infants were born, but they all died, and in the Mughal system of succession his daughters could not inherit the throne.

Akbar was now twenty-six. With singular determination, he set out to assure the future. In his world there was no better way to do this than to visit shrines, seek the counsel of holy men, pray, and give alms to the poor. Anxiously he made pilgrimages and beseeched living saints, convinced that their blessings might speed his wishes. In the midst of his search, a Muslim holy man came to his attention. This was Shaykh Salim ud-Din Chishti, whose fame had been spreading throughout the land. Akbar quickly arranged to visit him.

The eighty-year-old shaykh was a member of the Chishti order, a religious brotherhood known for a pure, austere lifestyle. His hermitage lay on the large rocky outcrop at Sikri, a site with connections to previous Mughal rulers. It was there, beneath that rock, that Babur rowed on a lake and created a Garden of Victory. It commemorated his defeat of the Rajput Rana Sangram Singh at Khanua, just ten miles to the west. Babur worked on his memoirs in the shade of that very garden. Humayun knew this place as well. He rested here one night while fleeing Hindustan.

The day came for Akbar's visit. The anxious young emperor approached barefoot as a sign of humility. He bowed to the shaykh and begged for his blessing. In response the white-bearded holy man uttered a prophetic vision of the future. The emperor was not to worry, he assured him, all would be well. He would have not one son but three, all within a short time.

Not long after that, Akbar's Rajput queen, Maryam az-Zamani, became pregnant. Taking no chances Akbar quickly raised a house

THE BIRTH OF PRINCE SALIM, *ca. 1590, painted by Kesu Kalan, coloring by Ram Das, from the* Akbarnama. *Courtesy the Victoria and Albert Picture Library, London.*

This painting shows the great rejoicing when Akbar's first son, Prince Salim, was born. At the top, within the harem, Salim's mother lies in bed while the baby is held by a noblewoman. Below, outside the harem's walls, musicians play an energetic fanfare on drums, reeds, and horns. To their right, a woman accepts a large plate of food, perhaps a rice dish, from the imperial kitchens. At bottom left, just above the dark wall, a member of the court throws coins to the waiting populace. Money was distributed to the people on all great occasions, and this was one of the greatest for the young dynasty.

for his expectant wife next to the shaykh's hermitage at Sikri. There, she would be under the holy man's protection. Day by day she grew bigger with child. Would it be a son?

It was. On August 30, 1569, a boy was born to the proud queen. In gratitude to the shaykh, the child was given his name, Salim. Thirty-six years later he ascended the throne and took the title Jahangir, the "Seizer of the World." A short time after Salim's birth, two more boys were born to different wives. They were Prince Murad, born in 1570, and Prince Daniyal, born in 1572.

Akbar was overjoyed. The succession was now assured, and with it the future of the empire. In honor of these great events and the holy shaykh himself, Akbar resolved to "give outward splendor to this spot which possessed spiritual grandeur." He ordered work to begin on a new palace city in 1571 and named it Fatehabad, the "City of Victory." Years later it became known as Fatehpur, which has the same meaning. Today the name is linked to the original village of Sikri to form Fatehpur Sikri.

The Vision of Fatehpur Sikri

The splendid gateway that Akbar built in 1573 sat upon Sikri's highest ridge and faced south. Called the Buland Darwaza, the "Lofty Gate," it formed a magnificent entrance to Akbar's imperial mosque. Like the rest of the city, it was built of the local red sandstone, but was inlaid as well with costly white marble. The Buland Darwaza was truly lofty, rising higher than a modern thirteen-story building. It thrust massively upward to overlook the town and its surrounding countryside below. It was a gateway of triumph, raised to celebrate a significant victory, the conquest of Gujarat. This wealthy western province borders on the Arabian Sea, and its ports had a valuable trade with the West.

At the center of the gateway, an immense pointed arch led inward to the sacred precincts. On either side gracefully carved inscriptions

Kabul
Peshawar
KASHMIR
PUNJAB
Lahore
Kandahar
Indus River
Delhi
Agra
RAJPUTANA
Yamuna R.
SIND
Benares
Allahabad
Ganges River
MALWA
GUJERAT
KHANDESH
BENGAL
Bombay
GOLCONDA
Gulf of Bengal
Sea of Oman
Goa
Calicut
CEYLON
Colombo

1561–1605

Mughal Empire on the death of Akbar in 1605

◆ European trading posts

△ Forts

0 100 200 300
Miles

AKBAR'S EMPIRE
AT HIS DEATH

climbed its entire length, their text chosen by Akbar himself. It was a key to the dual nature of this city, for Fatehpur Sikri was both a glittering imperial capital and spiritual center. The text reflected Akbar's complex nature as well.

One set of inscriptions expressed Akbar's greatness as lawgiver,

GENERAL VIEW OF FATEHPUR SIKRI, *old postcard.* This view, taken in the early part of this century, shows the area of the former imperial harem. To the left is the Panch Mahal, a stepped, five-storied pavilion in which the women of the harem enjoyed cool breezes and views of the lake. To the right and beyond is a building now called Jodh Bai's Palace. Legend says that it was the residence of the Princess of Jodhpur, Akbar's wife, but scholars think that it might have been Akbar's sleeping quarters.

JALI. *Photograph courtesy the American Institute of Indian Studies, Varanasi.* Jalis were carved stone screens that were used in Indian palace architecture. They allowed cool breezes to circulate through rooms—so important in India's hot climate—while ensuring privacy. Some of India's most beautiful jalis are found in Fatehpur Sikri.

BULAND DARWAZA, FATEHPUR SIKRI. *Photograph courtesy the American Institute of Indian Studies, Varanasi.* Buland Darwaza, which means "Lofty Gate," is the entrance to Fatehpur Sikri's imperial mosque. The gate rises up over the village below and stands higher than a thirteen-story building. It is one of the most impressive monuments of Akbar's reign, built to commemorate his conquest in 1573 of the wealthy western province of Gujarat, on the Arabian Sea.

mighty warrior, and builder. It celebrated his triumphs over Gujarat in strong poetic language. The other set revealed the inner man, concerned with life's deeper purpose. It was a quote from the Holy Quran.

> Jesus Son of Mary (on whom be peace) said:
> The World is a bridge, pass over it, but build no houses upon it.
> He who hopes for an hour may hope for eternity.
> The World endures but an hour.
> Spend it in prayer, for the rest is unseen.

The very emperor who erected this overpowering gate had selected a quote that questioned the need for permanent things. That was Akbar's dual nature, a dynamic builder of states and cities, yet happiest when immersed in philosophic thought.

During the city's years of active use, it functioned as the head of the empire. The emperor gave audience twice daily. Justice was administered, ambassadors received, and battles planned. Nearby Agra held the overflowing Mughal treasury within its impregnable walls. In the unlikely case of an invasion, Fatehpur's residents could flee there for safety. The road between the two cities was constantly crowded with members of the court, merchants, artisans, and peasants. In 1584 the English merchant Ralph Fitch took this road to the new capital and reported: "All the way is a market of victuals and other things, as full as though a man were still in a towne, and so many as if a man were in a market." Today that roadway scarcely sees the traffic it once held four centuries ago. In Fatehpur Sikri's heyday, it was a twenty-four-mile-long bazaar crowded with nobles in their *palki,* or hand-carried litters, gilded carts, barefoot holy men, miles of food stalls, shops of silk merchants, and sellers of gems.

The palace city at the top of the ridge also housed the imperial mosque. This was the first part of the city to be built, and it lay over the site of the shaykh's hermitage. The mosque's vast courtyard sheltered the tomb of Shaykh Salim ud-Din Chishti, who had died in 1572, the year that Prince Daniyal was born.

Akbar's son, Jahangir, related in his memoirs how the dying shaykh made a request that typified the spirit of Akbar's reign. He asked for Tansen, the court's brilliant Hindu musician, to come and sing for him. As the renowned Tansen sang, the shaykh approached his death. He summoned Akbar and Prince Salim to his bedside. Placing his own turban on Salim's head he gave him his final blessing.

Today, as in Akbar's time, the shaykh's beautiful white marble tomb is a center of pilgrimage. Those who desire children ask the shaykh's blessing, and they leave tied threads on his shrine as tokens of their visits. Each year a great festival celebrates the anniversary of the saint's death. Food is offered, lights kindled, and sacred poems called *qawwalis* are sung.

The Mughals had taken possession of Hindustan only forty-five years earlier, yet Akbar's capital looked completely at home there. Lacy *jalis,* filigree-patterned stone screens, were inset into windows and corridors. These might have been crafted by artisans from the western province of Gujarat, whose finest buildings bore intricate, exquisite carvings. Deep carved overhangs called *chajjas* gave shade and protection from the monsoon's annual rains. *Chattris,* the small domed pavilions, crowned various buildings, and most of the palace was constructed according to the post and beam technique, a native style. Even the city's predominant color, earthy red sandstone, was uniquely Hindustani.

Fatehpur's palaces were set around small garden courtyards that were unmistakably Muslim in feeling. There was no one grand building but rather a succession of airy pavilions grouped around fountain-filled courtyards and gardens. Breezy arcades swept under deep overhangs, and pillared halls overlooked the countryside below. The palace complex was set onto the hillside and small flights of stairways connected its many levels.

Approaching Fatehpur Sikri along the busy road from Agra, the traveler of Akbar's day eventually reached the impressive Agra Gate. This was one of the many that pierced the eleven-mile circuit of walls guarding the city. The route through the Agra Gate led straight through a series of planned bazaars, and finally to the rear of the palace complex, but according to some scholars, this was not the main approach to the city. That way followed a far more beautiful route, skirting the walls until the broad, shimmering expanse of the lake opened up to one side. On the other, the city rose upon its hill, a mass of pavilions, gardens, and blue-tiled roofs.

The visitor on this path passed a curious round tower called the *Hiran Minar*, or "Deer Tower," a round, sixty-foot-high structure, bristling with stone spikes like the tusks of an elephant. Nearby was a huge serai, or inn, filled with merchants, travelers, and goods from all over the empire. Just beyond was the *maydan*, a large field where polo games and public events were held. Finally, the road approached a grand, ceremonial gateway leading up to the areas reserved for Akbar and his nobles. This gateway, flanked by two massive carvings of elephants, was the *Hathi Pol*, or "Elephant Gate." Above it was the "House of the Kettledrum," where an orchestra that included twenty pairs of kettledrums performed throughout the day and night.

The palace complex atop the hill consisted of many buildings, and scholars are still trying to learn more about how these buildings were used. In some cases they are even unsure of their original names. These beautiful sandstone buildings were the setting for Akbar's magnificent court during Fatehpur Sikri's brief life.

High on the hill's crest was one of the great public spaces, the *Diwan-i 'Am*. Here, in the Hall of Public Audience, the emperor saw large groups of nobles daily, sat in judgment, had receptions, and sponsored assemblies of prayer. Beyond this was the private complex of Akbar's palace. It had a Persian name, the Daulatkhana, which meant the "Abode of Fortune."

Within this area was a courtyard with a huge outdoor game board where Akbar and his nobles played *chawpar*, a game similar to Parcheesi. Women from the harem were used as the game pieces, and they moved to the players' commands. Not far from there, in another courtyard, was a large square pond with a stone island in the middle, the Anup Talao. Akbar once drained the pond and filled it with gold, silver, and copper coins from his vast treasury.

Overlooking this area stood a curious building that has been named the Panch Mahal, the Palace of Five Levels. It rose, steplike, with each level progressively smaller. It is now open on all sides, but some speculate that each level was once completely enclosed within delicate jalis. Although its exact function is unclear, many feel that the Panch Mahal could have been a part of the harem. With its position high on top of the ridge, its screened-in galleries would have caught the passing breezes and offered pleasurable views of the lake.

Fatehpur was a lakeside city back then. It is hard to imagine how utterly different it must have been. The lake has long since dried up, but in Akbar's day it stretched for twenty miles and reflected the city in its shimmering waters. Scudding breezes brought cool winds to the palaces above, while leisure boats, carved and adorned, carried silk-veiled ladies from the harem. Garden palaces dotted its shores, and wildlife, especially migrating birds, nestled in its waters. During festival nights colored lights glistened in its darkened waters.

The transformation of the formerly barren site was amazing to Akbar's contemporaries. Qandahari, in his chronicle, the *Tarikh-i Akbari,* expressed this in the poetic language of the court:

> The lands which were desolate like the hearts of lovers . . . attained freshness, purity, splendor, and value. . . . Trees were grown in the environs which had formerly been the habitat of rabbits and jackals, and mosques, bazaars, baths, caravanserais and other fine buildings were constructed in the city.

In its heyday Fatehpur Sikri contained a large population. Below the southern edge of the palace ridge lay the town itself, surrounded by spacious walls. Sections of the walls still remain and give a sense of its once large area. The town's residents were mostly merchants, craftsmen, servants, and entertainers, who flocked to this center of power. One small section was called Shaytanpura, or Devil's Town. It was here that the courtesans had their quarters. Akbar had made it known that his noblemen were forbidden to frequent the area, but despite that many did. When he sent spies to record the names of the quarter's most frequent customers, he was shocked to see some of his highest nobles prominently listed!

City of Ceremonies

As Akbar's reign progressed, he sought to display his power in increasingly elaborate court rituals and ceremonies. Like Louis the Fourteenth of France, who later said, "I am the state," Akbar felt that he symbolized the power of the Mughal Empire. The way he lived put that into practice. Everything surrounding the emperor's public appearances became a spectacle that enhanced his image. The more these ceremonies elevated Akbar above the rest of humanity, the more magnificent the dynasty appeared. Like his impressive architecture, this was advertising as well. The message was the same: power, wealth, and glory. Here is a description from Badauni, Akbar's contemporary, of the spectacular reception that greeted a visiting ruler. As he arrived at the city's ceremonial entrance, this is what he saw:

> Five thousand elephants, some with housings of European velvet, and some with Turkish cloth of gold, and some with chains of gold and silver, and with black and white fringes hung on their heads and necks, were drawn up in a line on both sides of the road: also Arabian and Persian horses hung with golden saddles of like splendor. And between each pair of elephants they placed a car of cheetahs with golden collars, and coverings of velvet and fine linen.

The year was filled with great festivals. On festival nights the city was lit up by spectacular displays of fireworks and colored lights. Perhaps the grandest of these was the springtime celebration of Nauroz, the Persian New Year, which Akbar introduced in 1582. Some years the Nauroz celebrations lasted for up to eighteen days,

CELEBRATION OF THE
NEW YEAR AT THE COURT OF
SHAH JAHAN, *ca. 1645, from the*
Padshahnama, *folio 70 verso.*
The Royal Collection, Her Majesty
Queen Elizabeth II.
Although this scene comes
from the court of Shah Jahan,
Akbar's grandson, it shows the
festive entertainment for Nauroz, the Persian New Year.
Imperial dancing girls enter-
tain the courtiers while the
emperor's musicians accom-
pany them with trumpets,
reeds, stringed instruments,
and drums.

and all of the city's palaces were elaborately decorated with rich
hangings, artwork, and lights. Each night a different palace hosted a
party for the emperor. Groups of musicians and singers performed
while dancing girls captivated the assembled guests. In the palace
courtyards, tents of gold and brightly painted colors were erected
and golden thrones inlaid with emeralds and rubies set under them.

At Nauroz gifts were given to the emperor. Each noble set out an expensive array of offerings: jewels, luxurious vessels, precious weavings, and exotic objects. According to established custom, Akbar ceremonially accepted them all and then graciously gave back the items he didn't want. This was known as *pishkash*. In return Akbar sometimes scattered pearls and jewels, or tossed miniature silver fruits for his courtiers to catch. Nauroz was also the time when Akbar would hand out awards, elevate his nobles, and bestow the coveted robes of honor.

The emperor had introduced a new ranking system for the entire empire. Everyone who worked in the imperial administration now had a rank, and there were thirty-three different numbered grades. This ranged from lowly civil service employees all the way up to the imperial princes themselves. The numbers in the system corresponded to the old Mongol military system, where each commander was responsible for supplying a certain number of troops and horses. Even if you were a court artist, for instance, and had never fought in a war you still had a military ranking. The number ranks began as low as thirty-three and climbed to the stratospheric six thousand. Anyone with a ranking of five hundred or higher was considered a noble. Below that were the vast numbers of civil servants, artisans, soldiers, state-paid clerics, and so forth. Anyone below the rank of five hundred was paid by the state in cash.

For the nobles above five hundred there was a different system of payment. They were given gifts of land called *jagirs* and received their incomes through the tax revenues from these lands.

A *jagir* could be a group of villages or an entire province. Late in Akbar's reign a new ranking system for nobles was put into effect. Each noble was given two numerical ranks. The first was their salary level. The second represented the number of troops they actually had to supply to the imperial forces.

Unlike Europe, where nobles inherited their landed estates, none of the Mughal nobles owned their *jagirs*. They belonged to the emperor, and were changed approximately every two years so that nobles could not build independent power bases. Upon a noble's death his *jagir* reverted directly to the crown. Nobility was not hereditary, and while the children of nobles had distinct advantages, they could not inherit their parents' incomes or lands. Only the emperor could grant lands, monies, and rank, and frequently they were taken away if he was displeased with a noble. In addition, in order to discourage nobles from getting too attached to their lands, they were often shifted around the empire.

Akbar kept his nobles under control by punishing and rewarding them through grants of rank. The annual Nauroz awards ceremony was an eagerly awaited part of an ambitious noble's life.

The Emperor as Patron

Down the hill from the palace complex were the Karkhanas, the imperial workshops. There were at least one hundred of them, and it is estimated that they employed thousands of workers and artists. The Kharkhana area was like a large village in itself, with studios that turned out everything from elaborate guns and armor to luxuriant perfumes and clothing.

Akbar, with his immense physical energy and probing curiosity, loved to make things himself. One witness, the European priest Father Monserrate noted: "The king is considered by some to be mad, because he is very dextrous in all jobs, because I have seen him making ribbons like a lace-maker, and filing, sawing, and working very hard."

Indeed, it is said that Akbar invented a method of prefabrication so that the stone walls for Fatehpur could be precut and fitted off site. He was also keenly interested in the progress of the construction, and made inspections frequently.

The most exalted of Akbar's workshops was the Kitabkhana, the House of Books. This was a complex that housed the emperor's astounding library, spaces for scholars and translators, and all of the studios for book production. Within its walls worked the court's

**AKBAR INSPECTS THE BUILD-
ING OF FATEHPUR SIKRI,**
ca. 1590, from the Akbarnama.
*Courtesy the Board of Trustees,
Victoria and Albert Museum,
London.* Akbar took an active
interest in the construction of
his new city. Here he is shown
(top right, center) looking at a
workman performing his task.
Various construction jobs are
shown here, including carvers
working on the precut stone
panels (bottom right) and
mortar being made for
cementing stones in place.
(bottom left, center).

artists, gold leaf experts, calligraphers, scribes, and bookbinders. It was here that the emperor's magnificent manuscripts were produced: the *Baburnama, Akbarnama,* a huge number of illustrated tales, histories, sacred works, and books of poetry. Akbar was as great a patron as he was a collector. At his death his library contained approximately twenty-four thousand volumes, including works in Hindi, Persian, Greek, Latin, Arabic, and Kashmiri.

Life at Fatehpur Sikri

Akbar's amazing energy set the pace of life at Fatehpur. Everything was lively and almost bigger than life. Masses of colorfully dressed courtiers schemed, gossiped, and thronged its public spaces daily. They spoke Persian, Hindustani, the dialects of Central Asia, and even European languages. Proud, turbaned Rajput chieftains jostled white-robed, bearded Sufi shaykhs. Bare-chested Hindu priests sat near Persian dandies in bright silk robes. The most colorful was Akbar himself, who designed his own clothing, even down to his boots. Like his father, the emperor wore a different color for each day, the hue determined by the movement of the planets.

Wherever the emperor walked, an entourage of at least forty followed at all times. Jugglers, acrobats, and wrestlers performed at court every day. Their playful antics were a lively backdrop for the court's masterful singers, whose soulful voices accompanied lilting stringed instruments. At various times of the day and night, the court orchestra played from their hall above the Elephant Gate. The boisterous sound of their massed reeds, trumpets, and deep pounding drums was background music for the life of the city.

Magnificent awnings called *shamyanas* stretched overhead. Their colorful patterns offered shade from the sun's harsh rays. Beneath them lay woven gardens, fine carpets strewn with large, luxurious silk pillows for sitting or reclining. Servants poured wine from golden vessels while mangos, grapes, pomegranates, and endless types of dainty sweets sat on rare Chinese porcelain plates. Water gushed from many fountains; it sprayed, trickled, splashed, and flowed. The air was filled with precious scents and lovely sounds.

The palace walls were like gardens themselves, the cool stone carved with luxuriant foliage. There was no furniture as we know it. Beds, pillows, lanterns, and carpets were placed wherever they were needed by the armies of servants. Rooms served many functions, and because of the warm, dry climate, life was often lived out of doors. Chairs were never used. People ate, read, and slept on floors spread with beautiful carpets.

The Ibadatkhana

The only chair was the emperor's throne. The man who ruled from this priceless seat was the center of this glittering, ceremonial world. Akbar was immersed in the daily business of being Hindustan's emperor. But he also sought the spiritual mysteries of life. Badauni described how he would leave the palace and devote time to deeper issues: "In order to show his gratitude for some of his blessings, he would sit many a morning alone in prayer and mortification upon the stone bench of an old cell which lay near the palace in a lonely spot."

As Akbar searched he had philosophic works read to him, and looked forward to meeting with religious sages. In 1575 he created the Ibadatkhana, the House of Worship, as a place of religious debate and dialogue. A general proclamation was published throughout the realm. It was directed toward

> all orders and sects of mankind—those who searched after physical and spiritual truth, and those of the common public who sought for an awakening, and the inquirers of every sect. (*Akbarnama*)

They were invited to come to Fatehpur, where on Friday nights, "the night of illumination," after prayers at the imperial mosque, the discussions would begin.

At first, the Ibadatkhana hosted only Muslims. The participants were carefully seated along the four walls of the enclosure according to their affiliations. At that time Hindustan contained a diverse Muslim population with many different approaches to the faith. At one end stood members of the *ulama*, the state's salaried religious judges. These deeply conservative clerics were committed to established religious law. At the opposite pole were the highly mystic Sufis, who, influenced by Hindu philosophy, questioned the very nature of God and existence.

Perfumed incense filled the air as the discussions ground on until well past midnight. The emperor sat and listened intently to the debates, occasionally asking questions. Tempers ran high as the sages and clerics clashed over issues of belief.

Badauni related that at one point a member of the ulama flew into such a deep rage that the entire assembly turned into a raucous shouting match. An annoyed Akbar turned to Badauni and instructed him to report anyone who misbehaved. He would have them thrown out. Badauni whispered to a friend that if that were the case most of the group would have to be expelled. The emperor overheard him whispering and demanded to know what he said. When the cowed Badauni told him he burst out in gales of laughter and repeated it to everyone around him.

After three years Akbar grew disillusioned with the violence of the discussions, the name calling, threats, and insults. He was eager to examine other points of view and decided to invite non-Muslims. Soon the Ibadatkhana featured lively interchanges among Hindus, Parsis, Jains, Jews, and Christians. Badauni, in his history *Muntakhab al-Tawarikh*, reported: "Learned men of various kinds and from every country, and professors of many different religions and creeds assembled at his Court, and were admitted to converse with him. Night and day people did nothing but inquire and investigate."

Badauni himself was quite conservative and highly critical of the proceedings. For him, the inquiring and investigating were doing nothing but destroying the emperor's attachment to Islam. His his-

AKBAR PRESIDING OVER
DISCUSSIONS IN THE
IBADATKHANA, *ca. 1605, by Nar
Singh, from the* Akbarnama.
Chester Beatty Library, Dublin.
This shows a scene from
Akbar's religious discussions,
which were always held on
Friday nights. Akbar sits
cross-legged on a throne while
one of his three sons stands to
his right and an attendant fans
the emperor with a cloth. To
the left are two Catholic
priests in black, Fathers Aqua-
viva and Henriquez, and Muslim clerics.

tory of Akbar's reign was never published in his own lifetime. Its
critical comments would have placed his life in danger. It is ironic,
therefore, that his sadly disapproving description of Akbar's philosophy should be the best key to the emperor's feelings:

As a result of all of the influences which were brought to bear on his
Majesty, there grew, gradually . . . the conviction in his heart that

there were sensible men in all religions . . . and men endowed with miraculous powers among all nations. If some true knowledge was thus everywhere to be found, why should truth be confined to one religion?

The narrow limits of one religion were no longer enough for Akbar. He sought truth where he could find it. He turned increasingly toward Hinduism, fasting regularly, abstaining from meat, and drinking only water from the sacred Ganges. He visited Hindu holy men at their hermitages and accepted teachings from them. He began celebrating at court Hindu holidays like Diwali, the Festival of Lights. On occasion he even wore a *tilak*, a Hindu colored mark, on his forehead. In 1582 he placed the disgruntled Badauni in charge of the team that was translating the *Mahabharata* into Persian. The manuscript was then given over to the leading Hindu artists of the court, who painted beautiful illustrations for the text.

Akbar began adopting rituals from the Parsis, followers of the ancient Zoroastrian religion of Persia. He began worshiping the sun, and saluted it with prayers each dawn and dusk. He also introduced the worship of fire, symbol of divine light. As his reign progressed Akbar increasingly identified with images of the sun and of light.

In 1582 he founded a kind of mystical brotherhood called the Din-i Ilahi, the "Divine Faith." The band was largely drawn from the members of the court and included both Muslim and Hindu nobles. Like the European knightly orders, it had ceremonies of initiation and secret insignia. Members took a vow not to kill, except in battle or the hunt. The insignia included a small portrait of the emperor worn by its members. Its rituals gave reverence to the sun and hailed the divinity of light.

Around this time the first Europeans began arriving at the Mughal court in Fatehpur Sikri. In 1580 three Roman Catholic priests arrived from Goa, the Portuguese colony on India's west-central coast. They had been invited by Akbar, who was interested in learning about their foreign beliefs. They were formally presented in a ceremony at court and had brought the emperor a valuable gift, Europe's newest and most lavish printed edition of the Bible, a seven-volume set with many illustrations.

When the priests' gift was presented, Akbar solemnly kissed each volume, and then put each briefly atop his head. Since the head was felt to be the highest, most sacred part of the body, Akbar's action exhibited his veneration and profound respect. Akbar was so impressed with the priests that he sent his son Murad to study their religion and language. He paid many visits to their chapel and invited them to participate in the discussions of the Ibadatkhana. They were eager to convert the emperor to their faith and enthusiastically joined the debates.

One of the priests, Father Monserrate, left many descriptions of life at Fatehpur and of Akbar himself. He described the emperor as

> of good stature, sturdy body, arms and legs, broad-shouldered. The configuration of the face is ordinary and does not reflect the grandeur and dignity of the person because, besides being Chinese-like as the Mughals usually are, it is lean, sparse of beard, wrinkled and not very fair. The eyes are small but extremely vivid and when he looks at you it seems as if they hurt you with their brightness, and thus nothing escapes his notice, be it a person or something trivial, and they reveal sharpness of mind and keenness of intellect.

Because of his extraordinary energy and intelligence, Akbar was held in awe by his subjects. Yet, as Father Monserrate also pointed out, he maintained a cheerful presence with the public while retaining his imperial dignity.

The Final Days

Fatehpur was abandoned in 1586, when the capital was moved to the northern city of Lahore, in the Punjab. The northern areas of the

THE DEPOSITION FROM THE CROSS, *ca. 1598. Courtesy the Board of Trustees, Victoria and Albert Museum, London.* European art brought by the priests who visited Akbar's court made a tremendous impression on court painters, who promptly made copies of the new art. From European art they began to incorporate landscape elements, figure drawing, and techniques of perspective into their work. Mughal art became a unique combination of Persian, Hindustani, Central Asian, and European influences. This painting was based on an original by the Italian painter Raphael.

WESTERN ART

Akbar's court artists soon expressed great interest in the artwork the priests brought. Within their chapel were many religious paintings, and the Bible was placed in the Kitabkhana, where they worked. Akbar's European visitors opened a new era in Mughal art. The artists soon made copies of the foreign artworks and learned about European methods of figure drawing, perspective, and landscape painting. The European emphasis on realistic depiction combined with the Mughal love of nature to produce an entirely new style. Portraiture, although present in the Hindu and Persian traditions, took on a new emphasis and became a brilliant component of Mughal imperial painting.

empire had become troublesome, and Akbar needed to be closer to the center of military activity. The entire court departed Fatehpur with the emperor. When he finally returned to central Hindustan in 1598, Akbar reinstated Agra as his capital, and left Fatehpur behind.

Akbar's abandonment of the city he had so lovingly created remains one of the puzzles of his reign. The classic explanation, and one advanced as early as 1608 by European travelers, was that the city's water supply had failed. While this may have been partially true, it does not explain why Fatehpur's palace continued to be used by Akbar's successors until 1658. It is said that Akbar's own courtiers were surprised that the emperor chose Agra rather than Fatehpur to return to late in life.

Some speculate that Fatehpur's association with the memory of the sainted shaykh discouraged Akbar from returning there. By the end of his reign, they reason, he felt increasingly distant from the

Muslim orthodox world represented by the revered shaykh's cult. Others say that Agra was far better defended, more able to withstand the turbulence of Akbar's last years. His son Salim had rebelled and threatened to march on his father's forces. With that possibility Agra was a more secure base. Another, more personal reason is that Akbar might have felt saddened by the memory of a city built to celebrate the birth of his sons. All three had turned out to be severe disappointments to him.

Akbar died in 1605, after an incredibly long reign of forty-nine years. Unfortunately his last years were not happy ones. While Akbar was fighting in the Deccan in 1601, his eldest son, Salim, rebelled against him. Eager for the throne that his father still occupied, Salim set up his own court at Allahabad and even began to mint his own currency. Eventually he gave up the rebellion and was reconciled with his enraged father. Akbar was disillusioned with his son, but he had no other choice for an heir. All three of his sons had become alcoholics and only Salim was left. Princes Murad and Daniyal had drunk themselves to death in the last years of his reign.

As Akbar lay dying of dysentery, intrigues over the succession swirled around him. Many wanted to pass over the thirty-six-year-old Prince Salim in favor of his son, Khusrau, then seventeen. An extraordinary meeting of the nobles was called, and the majority decided for Prince Salim. He was to become the next emperor, Jahangir.

Akbar was buried in a magnificent tomb at Sikandra, near Agra. The building was built after his death by Jahangir. Sikandra was unusual even for its time, and there is nothing else in India that resembles it. It is tiered like a pyramid, and Akbar's tomb lies on the very highest level.

The English traveler William Finch visited Sikandra a few years after Akbar was buried there. The tomb still wasn't completed when he arrived there. Then as now, the building lay within extensive gardens set with elaborately tiled entranceways. He described the place this way:

Here within a fair round coffin of gold, lies the body of this monarch, who sometimes thought the world too little for him. The tomb is much worshipped by Muslims and Hindus, who regard him as a great saint. . . . By his head stands his sword and shield, and on a small pillow his turban, and nearby two or three beautiful gilded books. . . . At his feet stand his shoes. . . . Every one approaching makes his reverence and puts off his shoes, bringing in his hand some sweet smelling flowers to strew on the carpets or to adorn the tomb.

In death, as in life, Akbar was revered by his subjects, no matter what their religious background. He had achieved one of his deepest goals, being an emperor for all of his people.

Chapter 7

NUR UD-DIN MUHAMMAD JAHANGIR

An Imperial Puzzle

Jahangir was a fortunate ruler. Akbar, his father, made the empire great; he had only to maintain it and the rest would take care of itself. In fact, he succeeded beyond his father's expectations. His reign witnessed unprecedented peace and continued prosperity.

Still, Jahangir was a complex puzzle of contradictory parts. He sought the company of holy men, but was addicted to pleasure. He worshiped the memory of his father, but plotted his best friend's murder. Although good-natured, he could fly into sadistic rages. His character was noble and at the same time weak. Jahangir was elusive, the most intriguing Mughal by far.

Above all else Jahangir loved beauty. He created it in his surroundings, inspired it in his artists, and sought it in love. One of his life's greatest passions was his empress, Nur Jahan, a Persian noblewoman of legendary beauty. Unlike his father, so active and ambitious, Jahangir preferred to savor life's pleasures. He reveled in the world of the senses, as this description of a journey reveals:

JAHANGIR PREFERRING A SUFI SHAYKH TO KINGS *(detail), 1615–18, by Bichitr. Freer Gallery of Art, Smithsonian Institution, Washington, D.C.*

On Thursday the sixth of the month the halting place was at Hatya. On this road many palas-trees were in blossom. This flower, too, is peculiar to the jungles of Hindustan; it had no scent, but its color is flaming orange. The base of the flower is black, the flower itself is as big as a red rose. It is so beautiful that one cannot take one's eyes off of it. As the air was very sweet and the clouds had hidden the sun, and rain was gently sprinkled about, I felt an inclination to drink wine. In short, this road was traversed with great enjoyment and pleasure.

This excerpt is taken from Jahangir's own memoirs, a book fully as extraordinary as that of his great-grandfather, Babur. They were the only Mughal rulers to commit their private thoughts to paper, but their works are quite different. The *Baburnama* is lively and down to earth, a frank, rollicking tale of his many adventures. Jahangir's book, on the other hand, balances calm regal dignity with a personal, almost intimate tone. His memoirs, the *Tuzuk-i-Jahangiri*, are a direct window into his fascinating mind. To read his memoirs is like being aboard a barge on a slow-moving river. Everything that passes by is noticed in leisure and carefully observed. Thoughts flow easily from events to perceptions to opinions to notations of his day at court.

Like Babur, Jahangir enjoyed nature and keenly observed it. Jahangir, for instance, kept a pair of wild cranes. He named them after the legendary lovers Laila and Majnun and followed their lives over the course of the years. After they mated he observed their vigil of guarding the eggs:

The female used to sit on the eggs the whole night alone, and the male stood near her on guard. It was so alert that it was impossible for any living thing to pass near her. . . . When the sun illuminated the world with his rays, the male went to the female and pecked her back with his beak. The female then rose, and the male sat in her place. She returned and in the same manner made him rise, and seated herself. In short the female sits the whole night, and takes care of the eggs, and by day the male and female sit by turns. When they rise and sit down they take great precautions that no harm shall come to the eggs.

JAHANGIR AND HIS FATHER,
AKBAR, *ca. 1630, by Balchand,
from the Kevorkian Album. Metropolitan Museum of Art, New York.*
In Akbar's later years his relationship with Jahangir was
full of disappointment and bitterness, yet this painting sug-
gests otherwise. Jahangir
commissioned this painting
long after Akbar had died, and
it expresses the reverence that
he felt for his father after his
passing.

Like Babur, Jahangir paid homage to his father in his memoirs.
Jahangir was elaborate in his praise, for he clearly considered Akbar
to be almost superhuman. "The good qualities of my revered father
are beyond the limit of approval and the bounds of praise," he wrote.
"In his actions and movements he was not like the people of the
world, and the glory of God manifested itself in him." Throughout
his memoirs Jahangir often evoked the blessed memory of his father.

Yet, when Jahangir was still Prince Salim, he caused Akbar
exceptional anguish. He rebelled against him and set up his own capital at Allahabad, about 350 miles from Agra. Even worse, three

years before his father died, in 1602, he engineered the murder of his father's best friend and adviser, Abu'l Fazl. It was one of the paradoxes of Jahangir's character that he could both love his father and hurt him so deeply. But it was also a symptom of the problems Mughals had in determining who would rule when the emperor died. This issue would bring tragic consequences for the next reign.

Jahangir's Addictions

Jahangir spent his entire adult life under the influence of alcohol and *ma'jun*, or opium. For the Mughals, social drinking and taking stimulants were part of their ancient tradition. In their tradition men and women socialized separately, and drinking was an important element of male bonding rituals. Despite Islam's strong prohibitions on taking intoxicants, it was an accepted part of the Mughals' culture. In his memoirs Babur recounted many occasions when he participated in drinking parties, or took opium with his companions. Humayun was heavily addicted to opium, at least in the first part of his reign, and even Akbar took wine and opium on occasion. The difference was that Akbar could control his intake. Jahangir tried to, but ultimately could not.

> I myself drink wine, and from the age of eighteen years up till now, when I am thirty-eight, have persisted in it. When I first took a liking to drinking I sometimes took as much as twenty cups of double-distilled spirit; when by degrees it acquired a great influence over me I endeavored to lessen the quantity, and in the period of seven years I have brought myself from fifteen cups to five or six.

Jahangir's frank entries in his diaries detailed his struggles with alcohol. Yet one of the first laws he published stated that "no one should make wine or rice-spirit, or any kind of intoxicating drug, or sell them." Periodically the emperor would try to stop his drinking, but in the end his addiction won out.

THE EMPEROR'S FOUR NAMES

A Mughal emperor had three different names, usually Persian or Arabic in origin. These were his birth name, the name he took upon his accession to the throne, and an honorary name bestowed on him after he died. Jahangir was born as Prince Salim. *When he became emperor, he chose the name* Nur ud-Din Muhammad Jahangir. *Nur ud-Din means "the light of the faith," while Jahangir means "seizer of the world." He chose this name because, in his words, "the business of kings is the controlling of the world." After Jahangir died he was given the honorary name* Jannat-Makani, *which means "placed in paradise." Finally he had one more name, the affectionate* Shaykhi Baba, *a name his father used to call him as a child. Baba is a Hindustani term of endearment that means "father." Shaykhi referred to Shaykh Salim ud-Din Chishti, the holy man for whom Jahangir had been named.*

The English traveler William Hawkins spent time at Jahangir's court between 1609 and 1611 and was even one of his drinking companions. He described a typical night after Jahangir entered his private chambers.

> In this place he drinks five cupfuls, which is the portion that his physicians allot him. This done, he eats opium, and then he arises and being in the height of his drink lies down to sleep. . . . After he has slept for two hours, they awaken him and bring his supper to him; at which time he is not able to feed himself, but it is thrust into his mouth by others; and this is about one o'clock, and then he sleeps for the rest of the night.

Hawkins was eventually dismissed from court. During one of Jahangir's attempts to become sober, he prohibited anyone to come to court with liquor on his breath. The Englishman, fond of drinking himself, was found to smell of alcohol, and Jahangir promptly had him turned away.

Jahangir's Character

Jahangir could be quirky, and sometimes, when he was drunk, impulsively cruel. On one occasion, while hunting, three attendants accidentally got in his way just as he was about to shoot. Infuriated, he had one killed on the spot and the other two maimed. It is said

TRAINED ELEPHANTS EXECUTING AKBAR'S PRISONERS, *ca. 1590, from the* Akbarnama. *Courtesy the Board of Trustees, Victoria and Albert Museum, London.* One of the forms of Mughal capital punishment was to be crushed to death by specially trained elephants. This scene from the *Akbarnama* shows the grisly executions taking place.

that he had one of his officers flayed alive in his presence and yet another castrated as punishment. After the rebellion of his own son he had Khusrau's chief supporters impaled on stakes set alongside a road. Then he had his son placed on an elephant and driven down the road so that he could witness their gruesome fate.

While this seems cruel, it is important to remember that severe punishment was common at that time in Europe as well as in the Mughal Empire. In the Mughal court, Tuesday was the day of justice. Crime and rebellion were dealt with most harshly, and sentences included being impaled, crushed by elephants, flayed alive, or beheaded. There were even towers built along the main roads that displayed the severed heads of criminals. Akbar himself once had a servant put to death simply for falling asleep on his job. The Mughal emperors had absolute power, and their whims were speedily executed by their attendants.

Jahangir more than offset his occasional cruelty by his sensitivity. Upon the death of his pet antelope, he erected a beautiful pavilion in her memory. When his four-year-old grandson Shah Shuja was narrowly saved from death he wrote: "When I saw him in this state my senses forsook me, and for a long time, holding him in my affectionate embrace I was distracted with this favor from God."

Jahangir's intentions toward his subjects were noble, and he emulated his father's generosity. From his palace at Agra, he had a long golden chain hung with sixty bells strung to a post by the river.

> After my accession, the first order that I gave was for the fastening of the Chain of Justice, so that if those engaged in the administration of justice should delay or practice hypocrisy . . . the oppressed might come to this chain and shake it so that its noise might attract attention.

It is not known how many people actually attempted to gain Jahangir's attention this way, but some feel that few actually did. Since their complaints would have questioned the integrity of powerful officials, they might have feared the consequences.

Jahangir, like his father, was intrigued by the Hindu world. He

IMPERIAL AGRA

Agra, one of the three capitals of the Mughal Empire, was one of the great cities of Asia. The emperors and their nobles embellished the city with palaces, gardens, mosques, and garden tombs like the I'timad ud-Daula and the Taj Mahal. During Akbar's reign and afterward, the city was officially known as Akbarabad, "The City of Akbar," but it was always commonly known as Agra.

This is Jahangir's description of the city: "Agra is one of the grand old cities of Hindustan. My father . . . founded a fort of cut red stone, the like of which those who have traveled over the world cannot point out. . . . The habitable part of the city extends on both sides of the river. . . . In the number of its buildings it is equal to several cities of . . . Transoxiana put together. Many persons have erected buildings of three or four stories in it. The mass of people is so great, that moving about in the lanes and bazaars is difficult."

The city was long, and because it was built so close to the banks of the Yamuna River it was shaped like a half moon. The west bank, where Akbar's Fort stood, had more residents than the other bank, and the bazaars were located there. Their stalls were filled with colorful, abundant produce, and when the court was in residence the vast bazaar area was crammed with people.

Boats plied the river, their prows fancifully decorated with carved elephant or tiger heads. For almost the entire length of the city, the river's banks were lined with stone and brick palaces set amidst gardens of lush flowers, shady trees, and sparkling fountains. The houses of the common people were built from mud and had flat thatched roofs, which often caught on fire. The city's hot, dry climate encouraged fires and Jahangir himself considered it unhealthy. Today Agra still contains many buildings from its splendid past, but most of its gardens and palaces are gone.

was fascinated by the holy men who wandered through his realm free of worldly possessions. One, named Gosain Jadrup, lived in a small cave and was visited on a few occasions by the great emperor. They would sit outside the cave and converse about the nature of life. Jahangir often took vows to abstain from killing or eating meat, inspired by Hindu practice. He followed Muslim devotions as well. At the important Muslim shrine founded by Akbar in the city of Ajmer, west of Agra, he personally kindled the fire under an immense cooking pot. Then he and his empress fed thousands of the poor with the *kichri,* rice and lentils, that had been cooked in it. This was an important act of charity, one of the Five Pillars of the Muslim faith.

The Imperial Patron

While Jahangir appreciated spirituality, his passions lay elsewhere. He was foremost a sensualist, in love with the beauty of the world. His greatest contribution was as a patron of the arts. As imperial prince he patronized court painters and maintained his own studios. After he ascended the throne, he inherited his father's large painting studios, and eventually reduced the number of artists working there. This enabled Jahangir to pay closer attention to his artists than both his predecessors and successors. He encouraged the development of their talent and individual styles.

One of those painters was Abu'l Hasan. The emperor regarded his talent so highly that he gave him the title Nadir az-Zaman, meaning "wonder of the age." Abu'l Hasan was the son of a Persian artist who came to Akbar's court. While still a prince, Jahangir took him under his wing.

> My connection [with Abu'l Hasan] was based on my having reared him. From his earliest years up to the present time I have always looked after him, till his art has arrived at this rank. Truly he has become the Wonder of the Age.

It is typical of imperial patrons to attribute their artist's talents to their own inspiring patronage. Nevertheless, Jahangir knew Abu'l Hasan for most of his life and did pay attention to his development. He wrote the following entry shortly after receiving a painting from Abu'l Hasan depicting his accession to the throne. The painting was designed to be the triumphant opening piece to his memoirs. "As it was worthy of all praise," he enthused, "he received endless favors." Jahangir rewarded court painters whose work he prized. In one case he even awarded one of his artists with an elephant, the equivalent of many years' salary. Yet, most of his artists earned low salaries and were considered servants of the court, like the artisans that worked in the various Karkhanas.

The Emperor's Eye

Jahangir boasted that his eye was skilled enough to identify the work of any Mughal artist living or dead. Whether this was sheer exaggeration is not known, but his words indicated his alert interest.

> If there be a picture containing many portraits, and each face be the work of a different master, I can discover which face is the work of each of them. If any other person has put in the eye and the eyebrow of a face, I can perceive whose work the original face is, and who has painted the eye and the eyebrow.

During Jahangir's reign gifts of paintings poured in from European emissaries eager to establish trading privileges. Like other Mughal emperors, Jahangir was not very interested in the Europeans' wares—except for their art. He was deeply fascinated by these new images and kept demanding more of them from the hapless traders. Their letters home were soon filled with desperate pleas for more paintings, anything to please the wealthy emperor.

Jahangir was proud of his new acquisitions and placed some of them in the near-sacred space behind his throne. His European visitors were pleased to see that images of the Madonna and Child hung behind the Great Mughal as he gave his daily *durbar*, or audience. What they didn't know was that the Mughals traced their own lineage to a miracle much like the virgin birth of Jesus. According to a legend, Jahangir's distant ancestor was a Mongol virgin princess who was impregnated by a divine ray of moonlight. Jahangir loved this European Christian image not only for its beauty, but its symbolic connection to his own auspicious ancestry.

The Europeans in turn were impressed by the skill of Jahangir's court artists. The English ambassador, Sir Thomas Roe, once presented Jahangir with a painting that he thought so excellent that it could not be copied. The emperor disagreed and invited Roe back that very evening. He was shown six identical paintings lying side by side in a candlelit room and asked to choose the original. Although he looked and looked, the astonished ambassador could not tell which one was his. Jahangir burst out into loud laughter, thoroughly delighted with his artists' success.

Kashmir

Given Jahangir's appreciation of beauty and of nature, it is no surprise that he fell in love with the empire's most exquisite province. Kashmir is a lake-filled valley that rests high up in northern Hindustan surrounded by snow-capped peaks. Akbar conquered it in 1586, and Salim joined him for the campaign. The cool, green valley soon worked its magic on both father and son. They considered it an earthly paradise and a delightful alternative to Hindustan's scorching summers. For Jahangir it was an escape. His asthma, worsened by his drinking, always improved there, and he could feast on the valley's beauty. His memoirs devoted page after page to Kashmir:

> If one were to praise Kashmir, whole books would have to be written.
> Kashmir is a garden of eternal spring . . . a delightful flower bed. Its

ZEBRA, *1620, by Mansur. Courtesy the Board of Trustees, Victoria and Albert Museum, London.* Jahangir's love for nature and curiosities combined in this portrait of a zebra brought from Abyssinia (now Ethiopia). It was painted by Mansur, whose masterful portraits of animals earned him the title *Ustad*, meaning master.

JAHANGIR PREFERRING A
SUFI SHAYKH TO KINGS,
*1615–18, by Bichitr. Freer Gallery
of Art, Smithsonian Institution,
Washington, D.C.*
This is one of the first paintings done by Bichitr, an artist
who recorded the splendor of
both Jahangir's and Shah
Jahan's reigns. This symbolic
picture was commissioned by
Jahangir to depict his pious
qualities as a ruler. Here he is
shown preferring the company
of a holy man over that of
kings. Bichitr used many
images from European art in
this painting: on the left,
below the white-bearded
shaykh, are the sultan of
Turkey and King James I of
England, both taken from
European portraits. Other
European images used are the
hourglass on which Jahangir
sits and the two angels
at bottom.

pleasant meads and enchanting cascades are beyond all description. There are running streams and fountains beyond count. Wherever the eye reaches there is greenery and flowing water. The red rose, the violet, and the narcissus grow of themselves; in the fields there are all kinds of flowers and all sorts of sweet-scented herbs, more than can be calculated.

Kashmir became the imperial Mughal summer capital. Each year the entire court and harem would make the long, sometimes arduous journey to this magical world. In between the ongoing business of the court, the emperor visited mountain valleys filled with spring flowers and breathtaking waterfalls. He took careful note of the multitude of flowers, their distinctive fragrances and characteristics. Then, as his great-grandfather would have done, he created new gardens. One, called Shalimar, became legendary, and remains so to this day.

Shalimar is located near Dal Lake, part of Kashmir's capital of Srinigar. Its setting takes advantage of the lake in the distance and snowcapped mountains behind. A lotus-lined canal leads from the lake up to the gardens, which are built on four broad, shallow terraces that subtly descend the hill. A central canal fed by an upper lake flows down through the garden, its waters cascading as they fall from each terrace. At the garden's heart stands a black marble pavilion surrounded by a large rectangular pool. All around the elegant pavilion, built by Jahangir's son Shah Jahan, fountains play and jets of water shoot upward, and the only way to reach it is to walk upon stepping stones.

With its mountainous backdrop, flower-filled terraces, cascading waters, and black marble pavilion, the Shalimar is the essence of romance. Sadly, it is not possible to go there today. Kashmir, so cherished by the Mughals, is now torn by violence. It is the victim of a complex civil war whose roots lie in the conflict between Muslims and Hindus. After Independence in 1947, Kashmir passed to the secular but predominantly Hindu government of India; yet its population was, and remains, overwhelmingly Muslim. Many, perhaps most of, Kashmir's people would prefer to be independent of both neighboring Muslim Pakistan and India. Yet Kashmir is so beautiful that neither nation can bear to let it go. In the process, Jahangir's "garden of eternal spring" is being destroyed.

In his day Kashmir was blissfully peaceful, a haven of tranquility that inspired only thoughts of beauty, and of love. It is likely that he walked among Shalimar's pavilions and flowers with the woman he cherished above all others, his empress Nur Jahan.

Nur Jahan was one of the most amazing women of her age, yet much of her life remains a mystery. Unlike her husband, she left no memoirs to tell her story. She spent her life in the world of the harem and emerged to history only through the words of others. She was capable and brilliant, so much so that she became the ultimate power behind the throne. Her husband willingly shared his power, and as he sank increasingly into his addictions, she wound up running the Mughal Empire.

Mihr un-Nisa

When the infant Mihr un-Nisa, the "sun of women," was born in 1577, her parents could have scarcely foreseen her brilliant future. They were impoverished and living in the remote border fortress town of Qandahar. The Persian Mirza Ghiyas Beg and his wife Asmat Begum were both from distinguished families, but they had to leave their native land. They were en route to the court of Akbar, where Mirza Ghiyas Beg hoped to find a position.

Mihr un-Nisa's father had the perfect credentials for a role at court, and he soon rose through the ranks of government service. He was so highly thought of that when Jahangir took the throne he awarded him a high rank and an exalted title, *I'timad ud-Daula*, the "pillar of the government."

It is safe to assume that Mihr un-Nisa was well educated in the high Persian culture of her parents, but beyond that there is little

NUR JAHAN DRINKING WINE,
ca. 1750, Rajasthan, Kishangarh;
11¼″ × 8½″. Los Angeles County
Museum of Art; gift of Mr. and
Mrs. Michael Douglas.
An idealized image possibly of
Nur Jahan, painted long after
she died. The sumptuous jewelry she wears gives some idea
of how women of the court
adorned themselves in Mughal
times. The palms of her hands
are stained red with henna to
beautify them, and she holds a
dainty wine cup and flask.

known about her early life. She entered the court's registers only
upon her marriage to another Persian emigré noble at the age of
twenty-five. Her husband was Ali Quli Beg Istajlu, a military man
who soon joined the forces of Prince Salim. For his accomplishments
and valor in battle, Salim gave him a higher rank and new title, *Sher
Afghan,* the "tiger slayer." Six years later, in 1605, Mihr un-Nisa had
her first and only child by him, a daughter named Ladli Begum.
Shortly after, Sher Afghan and his family were posted to Bengal.

Within two years Sher Afghan was killed in a fight with
Jahangir's forces. The widowed Mihr un-Nisa was brought back to
Agra and placed under the protection of a high-ranking female member of the court. At this point Mihr un-Nisa fully entered the luxurious world of the *zenana,* the imperial harem. It was a world unto
itself, where women could rise to the heights of power or spend their
lives forgotten. The harem was one of the foundations of the Mughal
imperial world. Behind its forbidding walls, the emperor's women
lived their entire lives.

The Zenana

The harem was the interior world, the palace's innermost part far
removed from its public spaces. Its intimidating walls and guarded
gates sheltered a world bursting with life, a beautiful complex of
palaces and exquisite gardens.

The imperial Mughal palace was a world of compartments, like an
elaborate box. Everything was strictly divided between public
realms and private ones, and the most private of all was the harem.
It was sealed off from all men but the emperor, his sons, his guests,
and lowly tutors and artisans. The principle of separation extended
to spaces within the *mardana,* the palace for men, as well. There was
the Hall of Public Audience, and that of the Private Audience. Yet,
by definition the mardana was more public than the harem, because
much of the emperor's business was conducted there.

The confinement of women into their own quarters was known as
purdah. It was an old institution predating the Mughals that was
common to both upper-class Muslims and Hindus. Although Muslims were more strict about *purdah*, it was considered a sign of prestige in both cultures. Most people simply could not afford the cost of
separating their women, keeping them from working, and maintain-
ing servants for them. *Purdah* conveyed both wealth and luxury. Its
ultimate expression was the imperial harem, where thousands were
supported by the emperor's wealth.

Even today in some parts of the Muslim world *purdah* is strictly
maintained. Unlike the intermingling found in the modern West,
men and women still lead separate lives in these more traditional cultures. This was all the more strictly enforced in Mughal times.

Elaborate precautions were taken to ensure that this separation
was maintained. Each day the harem's doors were closed at sunset
and sealed. Guards patrolled both inside and out, making sure that
no one entered or exited illegally. A scribe reported all who came and
went, and reports were submitted daily detailing the activities of the
inhabitants. Once a week a report was read to the emperor himself
in front of the assembled residents.

The Harem's Inhabitants

Who lived within the confines of this hidden world? The wives of the
emperor, first of all. His major wives maintained their own palaces
within the harem's walls. Their palaces, and those of others, helped
account for the profusion of buildings that made the imperial palaces
seem like small cities.

Jahangir had only seventeen wives, but even so, the harem was
still a populous place. Each wife brought her own ladies-in-waiting,
servants, and retainers. Depending on her rank, her staff might
include anywhere from twenty to one hundred people.

Then there were the sisters of the emperor, important personages

DALLIANCE ON A TERRACE,
*period of Jahangir, 1605–27,
attributed to Govardhan. Los
Angeles County Museum of Art.*
Lovers have been depicted
throughout the history of
Indian art. Some art historians
have suggested that this highly
unusual painting might depict
Jahangir and Nur Jahan
embracing. Others feel that
it is unlikely.

in their own right. With some exceptions they were forbidden to marry from the time of Akbar on, but they maintained impressive households, with bevies of slaves, attendants, and artisans to satisfy their every need. The emperor's mother maintained her own important palace as well. She was a figure who commanded powerful respect and even reverence. Frequently she was the sponsor of major family ceremonies, such as marriages or the circumcision of the imperial princes.

All of the imperial princes were raised within the harem, where they were fawned over from their earliest days. There they were tutored in all of their subjects, and learned the protocol of the court. Concubines—unmarried women trained in the arts of singing and dancing—lived within these walls as well. They performed at court ceremonies and also were available for the emperor's pleasure.

Female guards patrolled the inside of the harem. In the days of Akbar and Jahangir, some of these women were brought from as far away as Russia or Abyssinia, today's Ethiopia. They were Amazons, tall, strong, and armed, who must have made a startling contrast to the lithe, silk-clad women within. The harem had its own mosques, kitchens, artisans' shops, laundries, and service establishments, all of them staffed by special attendants, who swelled its population.

Finally there were the eunuchs, male servants who managed the harem and provided its chief contact with the outside world. Eunuchs were men who had been castrated at youth and then sold into service as guards or attendants. Because they were castrated they were considered the only men, besides the emperor, who could have safe access within the world of *purdah*. Mughal India was not the only culture to have a special place for eunuchs; the Chinese and the Ottoman Turks did so as well. There were even eunuchs in Europe, but these men were trained to be singers, called *castrati*. Although the practice died out by the early 1800s, many eminent European composers wrote music designed to be sung by castratis.

Many of the Mughal eunuchs were from Bengal, the eastern portion of the empire. Each princess and major wife kept a few eunuchs in her entourage who were often their confidants. Despite this, the eunuch's first allegiance was to the emperor, whose women they safeguarded. Their position was called *nazir*, which meant "guardian." They were a constant conduit of information and gossip, since they passed almost daily through the harem's gates.

Women from all over Hindustan and southern India lived within the harem. There were also women from Central Asia, Persia, the Ottoman Empire, Tibet, Russia, and even a few from Western Europe. Diverse religions and languages coexisted within its walls, and different forms of national dress as well.

The Interior World

François Bernier, the French doctor and traveler, lived in Hindustan between 1659 and 1667. He once entered the harem to treat a patient who was too ill to be moved outside of its walls. To prevent him from seeing anything, his head and body were covered with a huge Kashmiri shawl and a eunuch led him by the hand, as if he were blind. In his eagerly awaited description of these inner parts, he wrote:

> You must be content, therefore, with such a general description as I have received from some of the eunuchs. They inform me that the harem contains beautiful apartments . . . spacious and splendid, according to the rank and income of the females. . . . On every side are gardens, delightful alleys, shady retreats, streams, fountains, grottoes, . . . lofty couches and terraces, on which to sleep cooly at night. Within the walls of this enchanting place . . . the eunuchs speak with extravagant praise of a small tower, facing the river, with plates of gold . . . and its apartments are decorated with gold and azure, exquisite paintings, and magnificent mirrors.

Life inside the guarded walls was a mixture of luxury and boredom, intrigue and beauty. Most of its women had little direct contact

ZENANA SCENE, *period of Jahangir, 1605–27, artist unknown. Metropolitan Museum of Art, New York; Theodore M. Davis Collection; bequest of Theodore M. Davis, 1915.*
This painting is a window into the daily life of the Mughal harem. Jeweled ladies of the nobility and their attendants relax on beautiful carpets by a small fountain in a garden. Women play music, drink wine, chat, and leisurely recline. A small child, perhaps a young prince, sits adorned with jewels and is carefully watched over. It is a scene that conveys the ease and luxury of harem life.

with the emperor. Even if they did, a sexual liaison with the emperor was more an opportunity for advancement than a matter of romance. Lavish gifts of jewels, slaves, and even larger quarters were bestowed on those whom the emperor favored. If one was fortunate enough to give birth to a prince, the result could be great prestige and wealth. Chosen women were summoned by the eunuchs, ravishingly adorned and scented, and conveyed to the emperor's bedchamber.

For many women over the age of thirty that was no longer a possibility. In the culture of the times only women under the age of thirty were believed to possess sexual appeal. There were exceptions, like Mihr un-Nisa, who won the emperor's heart when she was a widow in her mid-thirties, but for most the likelihood that the emperor would notice them was small. Lives were spent in waiting, hoping for the summons. Gossip was rife and all quickly knew who was the recipient of the emperor's favor.

On the positive side, the harem was a community of protected women whose lives were well provided for. Some lived in quarters of the greatest beauty. Even today in the palaces of Delhi's Red Fort, built by Shah Jahan, there is a hint of the extreme luxury that surrounded this world. The palaces were jewel-like pavilions, whose carved arches and white marble walls sported elegant decorations. Streams flowed in marble channels through the airy pavilions and lush gardens while golden fountains cooled the air with their delicate spray.

Lovely sounds animated these precincts: the cool gush of water, and the song of the birds. There was the laughter of royal children at play and the soft-spoken babble of many tongues. Music, too, for here the women sang, played stringed instruments, and made rhythm with drums. They wore tiny silver bells that tinkled as they walked. The sound of prayer was heard daily, the chanting of the Quran, and the cadences of Hindu devotions. Poetry, gossip, servants' chatter, and the emperor's august voice—all sounded in a day within the *zenana*'s walls.

Then, too, there was the flash of jewels, so beloved by Hindustan's people. From the top of her head to her very toes, a woman of the harem was hung with jewels and precious baubles. She might have emeralds adorning her hair, while a pearl-studded gold hoop pierced her nose. Earrings of precious stones might have dangled from her ears, while glittering necklaces embraced her neck. Perhaps tiny bracelets of diamonds flashed on her arms, while rubies ringed her painted fingers. She could have worn a tiny mirror on her thumb, set with pearls, and, cocking her head, now right, then left, she might have studied herself throughout the day.

Each day her servants rubbed her skin with essences of herbs and luxurious oils as she came from her scented bath. As her long hair dried, sandalwood was burned to infuse her tresses with its sweet fragrance. Then pastes were applied to accentuate her beauty. For the eyes and eyebrows there was the black of collyrium. For her lips, the red of the betel leaf, and henna to mark her hands and feet. On her forehead was placed a brightly colored *bindi,* a round mark of devotion and beauty. To finish, her neck and feet were anointed with fragrant musk or ambergris, a blossom was laid in her hair, and she was given cloves to chew, to sweeten her breath. The day would be half over, but she walked in ravishing beauty.

Besides jewels and beauty, the ladies of the harem had other pursuits to occupy their time. Some of the harem's residents had business interests in the outside world. They owned trading ships, held property, and collected tolls from certain routes. Their business affairs were managed by the eunuchs who had unrestricted access to the outside world.

The Mughal emperors, who prized learning, encouraged their ladies to educate themselves, and the harem was filled with opportunities to do so. Within its walls scholars and tutors gave lessons in languages, literature, poetry, logic, philosophy, mathematics, astronomy, and calligraphy. Women became accomplished scholars and competitions were held to test their knowledge and skill. Most valued of all was poetry, one of the Muslim world's highest forms of art.

Some of the greatest ladies of the realm composed poetry. One of them was Mihr un-Nisa.

During the four years prior to her marriage with Jahangir, Mihr un-Nisa lived in the imperial harem as a lady-in-waiting to Ruqayya Begum, a noblewoman of extremely high rank. At some point in this period, she met the emperor. Some sources placed that meeting at the annual Mina Bazaar, the one held in the sixth year of Jahangir's reign.

The Mina Bazaar

The Mina Bazaar was a harem tradition during the great festival of Nauroz. Amid the holiday's colorful celebrations, it duplicated the lush offerings and lively atmosphere of a real bazaar, but set within the harem's walls. Unlike a real bazaar, all men were forbidden except for the emperor. Tradesmen's wives hawked luxurious wares from around the country, while the unveiled harem ladies strolled, shopped, haggled, gossiped, and enjoyed themselves. The emperor himself strode among the ladies, bargaining on behalf of some, flirting with others, and even engaging in conversation with the tradesmen's wives.

The Mina Bazaar was the perfect setting for the emperor to notice a beautiful face, and according to many sources Mihr un-Nisa was an exquisite beauty. The two met, Jahangir was captivated, and within two months they were married, on May 25, 1611. Mihr un-Nisa was thirty-four years old then, and the emperor was forty-two, so it was a match of two mature adults.

Nur Mahal to Nur Jahan

Her first title, given at the marriage, was Nur Mahal, the "light of the palace." Three years later in 1614, she was honored with the exalted title of Nur Jahan, the "light of the world." By then she had risen quite far in her husband's esteem, and her power had grown substantially. The *Iqbalnama-i Jahangiri,* a chronicle of the reign written by the courtier Mu'tamad Khan, described the empress thus:

> Day by day her influence and dignity increased. All of her relations and connections were raised to honor and wealth. No grant of lands was conferred upon any woman except under her seal. The emperor granted Nur Jahan the rights of sovereignty and government. Sometimes she would sit in the balcony of her palace, while the nobles would present themselves, and listen to her dictates. Coin was struck in her name. On all Imperial decrees receiving the emperor's signature the name Nur Jahan the Queen Begum [Lady], was jointly attached.

NUR JAHAN WITH A RIFLE, *1612–13, by Abu'l Hasan (Nadir az-Zaman). Raza Library, Rampur.* Jahangir was so proud of Nur Jahan's extraordinary skill as a markswoman that he had her painted with her rifle by one of his favorite artists, Abu'l Hasan, the "Wonder of the Age." Some feel that this is the only authentic portrait of the empress taken from life. It shows just how singular Nur Jahan was, as few Mughal women were ever depicted with guns, much less hunting rifles.

Mu'tamad Khan's chronicle also reflected the growing jealousy of those who resented Nur Jahan's power. The author, who wrote "At last her authority had reached such a pass that the king was such only in name," never dared to publish his book during Jahangir's lifetime. It was only released afterward, when his son, no friend of Nur Jahan's, became emperor.

Jahangir relaxed his power into the hands of his capable wife. The queen was an impressive woman, and Jahangir her greatest admirer. Besides her ruling skills, she was reputed to have an abundance of talents, both great and small. She invented savory delicacies for the imperial kitchens and designed new styles of clothing. Her poetry was considered accomplished, and she helped design some of Kashmir's most celebrated gardens. In addition to all of this, she was extremely skilled at hunting. Jahangir described her amazing marksmanship on a tiger hunt:

> An elephant is not at ease when it smells a tiger and is continually in movement, and to hit [a tiger] with a gun from a litter is a very difficult matter. . . . Mirza Rustam, who, after me, is unequaled in shooting, has several times missed three or four shots from an elephant. Yet Nur Jahan so hit the tiger with one shot that it was immediately killed.

Nur Jahan soon began to assume the outward functions of an emperor. She used the title *Shahi,* meaning "Imperial," and rode out to great pomp and fanfare when she appeared in public. Many lavish buildings were erected in her name, a guarantee that her exalted reputation would spread. She decided who would receive the emperor's favor and reviewed all seeking advancement. Like an emperor, she accumulated a vast fortune, and as a good Muslim spent a significant part of it on charities. Her favorite gifts were dowries to poor orphan girls who otherwise could not marry.

The Quartet

Nur Jahan did not rule alone. She was part of a quartet that effectively governed the empire as the emperor fell more deeply into his addictions. Besides herself, the key players in this group were her father, I'timad ud-Daula, who had become the *wazir,* or chief minister of the empire. Then there was her brother Asaf Khan, who had held high posts in key provinces. Finally there was Prince Khurram, Jahangir's son. Khurram was by far the most capable of Jahangir's sons, and by common consent the one who was destined to succeed him on the throne. He would become the next emperor, Shah Jahan.

Together these four ran the empire for approximately nine years, beginning in 1611. They were linked by close family ties. Khurram married the beautiful daughter of Asaf Khan, Arjumand Banu. One day she would become Empress Mumtaz Mahal and the Taj Mahal would be built as her final resting place.

Although this family coalition ruled in apparent harmony, the seeds for its breakup were just under the surface. The increasingly absent Jahangir was the glue that held it all together. Nur Jahan's tremendous power derived from her being his wife. If he were to die, then his son would occupy the throne. Although Timurid women enjoyed tremendous power, there was no precedent for a woman to openly ascend the throne.

By 1620 the quartet began pulling apart. Khurram gradually slid into a rebellion against his father and soon became bitter enemies with Nur Jahan. They would never reconcile.

The End of Power

The years leading up to Jahangir's death were marked by a continuous succession of intrigues. These were instigated by the empress and her crafty brother as the question of succession loomed increasingly larger. Jahangir's chronic asthma was getting worse, and his slow but inevitable deterioration steadily proceeded.

Jahangir had once given his adored son Khurram the lofty title *Shah Jahan,* "emperor of the world." But as the emperor aged, he took to calling the prince *Bidaulat,* or "wretch." Khurram was in almost continuous rebellion four out of the last five years of his father's reign. As with Jahangir and Akbar, there was a reconciliation, or rather a surrender (Khurram's), in 1626. From then on all of the imperial family tensely waited, sides chosen up, for the end.

The emperor died on October 28, 1627, on the way back from his beloved Kashmir. Upon his death everyone immediately put their schemes for takeover into action. The winner was Khurram, backed by the skill and cunning of Asaf Khan. Nur Jahan gracefully accepted her defeat and was sent into enforced retirement at Lahore, the northern imperial capital. She was given a pension by Shah Jahan, and her daughter Ladli Begum joined her in exile. Neither Shah Jahan nor her brother ever made contact with her again. Little is known about her final seventeen years in Lahore. The same mystery that veiled her early years shrouded her later ones.

Nur Jahan died on December 18, 1645, and was buried in a modest mausoleum that she built for herself at Shahdara, near Lahore. Later on, her daughter was laid to rest by her side. Their tomb, which remains to this day, is set within gardens near Jahangir's impressive mausoleum.

I'timad ud-Daula's Tomb

This proud empress left a far more beautiful monument to posterity than her own modest tomb. It stands today in Agra, set within a garden on the banks of the Yamuna River. The building is called the I'timad ud-Daula, and is the tomb of her beloved parents, Mirza Ghiyas Beg and Asmat Begum.

The tomb is one of the most exquisite buildings in India, if not the world. It was started in 1622 and completed six years later. The empress lavished a fortune on its construction, an effort that employed an army of highly skilled artisans. What makes this building so amazing is the extraordinarily intricate ornamentation that covers every surface. It is as if the entire building were a Persian carpet, a magnificent swirl of rich designs colored with subtle tones of gold, tan, red, and brown on a pure white background.

I'TIMAD UD-DAULA'S TOMB, *1622–28, Agra. Photograph courtesy the American Institute of Indian Studies, Varanasi.* Nur Jahan built this jewel-like tomb for her parents in a riverside garden at Agra. Every inch of the white marble building is inlaid with delicate designs in semiprecious stones. This was the first building of its kind in Hindustan and one that pointed to the later Taj Mahal, just down the river.

MUGHLAI FOOD

Both Nur Jahan and Jahangir are supposed to have invented new dishes for the imperial kitchens. The luxurious tone of Mughal architecture, clothing, and jewelry was also found in its sumptuous food. Meals in the imperial palaces boasted a huge variety of exquisite dishes, served on rare Chinese porcelain, and platters of pure gold and silver. Today the northern Indian cuisine known as Mughlai comes directly from the heritage of the imperial Mughal kitchens. Like their art and poetry, the Mughals' food was influenced by the cooking of Persia, which was subtle and not very spicy. In time, the rich array of Indian spices entered their cooking and a new cuisine was formed.

Meats are a specialty of Mughlai cooking, and they are steamed in fragrant juices, marinated and roasted on skewers, and made into succulent little balls. Rice dishes are also prized, and one of the most opulent is the biryani, a layered meat and rice preparation. In Mughal times, such a dish would have been presented on elaborate golden platters, and it would have been decorated with crisp nuts, dried fruits, and sheets of silver thin enough to eat. The Mughals also loved sweets, and in addition to preparing fresh fruit sherbets, they also made a delicious form of ice cream called kulfi. In Hindustan's hot climate, kulfi, sherbet, and cooling drinks made with yogurt and fruits all helped to keep people luxuriously cool.

I'TIMAD UD-DAULA'S TOMB, *1622–28, Agra. Photograph courtesy the American Institute of Indian Studies, Varanasi.* A detail of the intricate *pietra dura* work on the exterior wall.

The background is the structure itself, a small, graceful building that resembles a jeweled box. The luxurious white marble was a material that Jahangir and Shah Jahan increasingly favored for their constructions. The walls are inlaid with the painstaking technique known as *pietra dura*, which requires the skill of a jeweler to execute properly. Semiprecious stones such as jasper, topaz, onyx, and carnelian are cut and individually polished. Then they are set into the intricate channels that have been cut into the wall and floor surfaces.

Nur Jahan's jeweled creation led the way to even greater masterpieces that would follow. Not far down the river, after it gently curves, lies a building that is known throughout the world. It was built by the man who became her bitter enemy, Shah Jahan. His reign marked a new height of Mughal splendor, and he left as his legacy the Taj Mahal. Like his father before him, he knew great love, and also deepest tragedy.

Chapter 8

SHAHIB UD-DIN MUHAMMAD SAHIB QIRAN SANI SHAH JAHAN

Gazing from the Terrace

It is easy to imagine that the elderly Shah Jahan might have looked forward to the late afternoons. By then Agra's harsh sun would have gently lowered toward the horizon. He would have stepped out onto the white marble balcony to catch the cool breezes. As evening prayers approached, the seventy-year-old former emperor might have gazed south down the curving river. Before him rose the domes of his beloved wife's resting place, golden in the day's dying light. He had called her Mumtaz Mahal, the "Chosen of the Palace."

He had built her exquisite tomb, the Taj Mahal, as a labor of love. There is a legend that she asked two things of him on her deathbed. The first was that he marry no one after her, and the second that he build her a tomb more beautiful than the world had ever seen. He did as she asked, and could now gaze on his masterpiece with pride and longing. It was so close that a bird could fly there and back in a moment's time. Yet Shah Jahan could not even walk there if he

SHAH JAHAN ON THE PEACOCK THRONE, *ca. 1630. Courtesy the Board of Trustees, Victoria and Albert Museum, London.*

wanted. He was a prisoner of his son Aurangzeb, locked within his own palace.

The tragedy that befell him swept the rest of his family to their destruction. His favorite son, Dara Shikoh, was murdered, and his other sons, Shah Shuja and Murad, had perished as well. Even Dara's son, his grandson Sulayman Shikoh, was imprisoned. It was rumored that in his cell he had been forced each day to drink the deadly opium potion *poust*, making for him a long, slow, but inevitable journey toward madness and death.

Shah Jahan's devoted daughter, Jahanara, joined him in his confinement, or perhaps she had no choice. In the family struggles she had chosen the losing side. Aurangzeb was the victor, who now ruled as the Emperor Alamgir from the imperial city that his father had erected at Delhi.

That city, Shahjahanabad, was an emblem of Shah Jahan's splendid reign. He had created a glorious setting for the dynasty. During his thirty-year reign, Mughal power stood supreme on the subcontinent. His court was fabled for its wealth and beauty. He sat upon a Peacock Throne so brilliant with jewels that its value was the stuff of legends. With such great accomplishments, how had this dreadful misfortune befallen him? What had gone so horribly wrong?

Baba Khurram

From the moment that he was born in 1592, everyone adored Prince Khurram. "Baba Khurram" they affectionately called him. Nurses cooed his birth name as they rocked him to sleep. It meant "joyous," for, as his father happily noted, "his advent made the world joyous, and gradually, as his years increased, so did his excellencies."

The little boy's greatest admirer was none other than his grandfather, Akbar. The emperor practically adopted the boy and gave him to be raised by one of his own senior wives, the devout

TAJ MAHAL SEEN FROM THE RIVER, *photograph by Luis Villela. Government of India Tourist Office, New York.*

TAJ MAHAL IN THE EARLY MORNING, *photograph by Luis Villela. Government of India Tourist Office, New York.*

ENTERING THE TAJ MAHAL, (opposite page), *photograph by Luis Villela. Government of India Tourist Office, New York.*

DETAIL OF CARVED FLOWERS
FROM EXTERIOR OF TAJ
MAHAL, *photograph by Luis
Villela. Government of India
Tourist Office, New York.*

Ruqayyah Sultan Begum. Years later she would take the widowed Mihr un-Nisa under her noble wing as well. Akbar and Khurram had a special relationship, and the emperor lavished affection on the child. Khurram soon displayed the promise that would mark him as easily the most capable of Jahangir's sons, destined for the throne.

His grandfather brought him along on his military expeditions and even accompanied him on his first day to school. Although the prince was three-quarters Rajput Hindu by descent, he was educated, like all imperial princes, as a Muslim. When the state's religious establishment fought to give him a strict Muslim upbringing, Akbar agreed. As an adult Khurram was more religiously conservative than either his father or grandfather.

Khurram grew up fawned over by his numerous attendants within the imperial harem. As a young child, he was dressed in the finest embroidered silks and adorned with jewels.

As Khurram grew he witnessed firsthand the drama surrounding the final five years of his grandfather's reign. He was with Akbar when his father rebelled against him. After their reconciliation the young prince took part in an unusual episode centered on an elephant fight. Many high nobles felt that Jahangir should be replaced in the succession to the throne by his first-born son, Khusrau. The aged Akbar, now in the last year of his life, was unsure of what to do and wanted an omen to point the way for him. He arranged for an elephant fight—pitting Jahangir's elephant against Khusrau's—a common imperial entertainment held at least once a week.

Akbar appointed his beloved Khurram, then twelve, to referee the portentous fight. Apparently Khusrau's elephant was about to win when Khurram, showing favor to his father, suddenly sent a standby elephant into the arena. This created much confusion, and rockets had to be fired off to separate the elephants. Khusrau's elephant panicked and ran away, making Jahangir the victor, thanks to his young son.

While the elephant fight presented an easy solution to the looming problem of succession, the reality was considerably harsher. Unlike

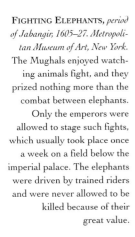

FIGHTING ELEPHANTS, *period of Jahangir, 1605–27. Metropolitan Museum of Art, New York.* The Mughals enjoyed watching animals fight, and they prized nothing more than the combat between elephants. Only the emperors were allowed to stage such fights, which usually took place once a week on a field below the imperial palace. The elephants were driven by trained riders and were never allowed to be killed because of their great value.

many European countries, where the throne passed to the oldest child, the Mughals had no given rule for selecting a new ruler. That meant that the imperial princes were forced to fight for the throne. These fights became full-fledged wars, which were very destructive to the empire. In the end, the strongest, or cleverest, of the imperial princes would become the next emperor.

Fortunately for the empire, Akbar did not have to face this. There were only half-brothers to challenge him, and they were easily dealt with. Jahangir was equally lucky. His two brothers died, and his only challenge was from Khusrau, who rebelled shortly after his father ascended the throne. The rebellion was soon put down, and Jahangir's reign enjoyed peace. Nevertheless, the critical problem of succession had not been solved. It would return many years later to haunt Khurram's reign as emperor, and bring terrible tragedy in its wake.

Arjumand Banu

One of the most important ceremonies in the early life of Prince Khurram was his marriage to Arjumand Banu in 1612. She was the niece of Nur Jahan, and the granddaughter of I'timad ud-Daula, the chief minister of the kingdom. Her father was Asaf Khan, who one day would become Shah Jahan's chief minister. Though Jahangir arranged the marriage, it was a union of love. Khurram had two other wives, strictly for political reasons, but his devotion was clearly to Arjumand Banu. He gave her the reverent name **Mumtaz Mahal** upon his accession to the throne.

MUMTAZ MAHAL *(detail of box), ca. 1900, northern India; opaque watercolor on ivory. Charles Wolfe Masters, Jr., and Family Trusts.* Like the idealized paintings of Nur Jahan, this painting of her niece, Mumtaz Mahal, came from the artist's imagination. There were almost no portraits of the empress taken from life, but her legendary beauty inspired artists to create images like this.

THE WEIGHING OF THE PRINCE

One of the ceremonies that Jahangir often noted in his memoirs was the annual weighing of the princes. Mughal emperors and imperial princes were weighed against precious metals for their birthdays. The ceremony was considered auspicious and blessed since the proceeds were given to the poor and holy men. During the ceremony the weighing was often repeated a number of times, with a fortune in bagged gold and silver piled onto the scales.

Members of the imperial family counted two birthdays each year. The first was the solar birthday, which corresponded to the Western calendar. The second was the lunar birthday, which followed the Muslim religious calendar. Since Akbar's time emperors had been weighed on both anniversaries, but princes were weighed only on their solar birthdays. Not Khurram. His adoring father decided that for his sixteenth lunar birthday he would be weighed as well.

Little is known about her, but some things can be guessed at with assurance. The first is that she must have been beautiful. Like his father, Khurram had cultivated tastes and a keen appreciation for beauty. Second, coming from her refined Persian family, she would have been well educated. Third, she was unusually devoted to her husband. In an atmosphere where imperial marriage was often a political arrangement, she shared completely in her husband's life.

Arjumand Banu traveled with Khurram wherever he went, even under very difficult conditions. Many feel that she was not just his wife, but his closest adviser as well. He gave her the seal of state to keep. All imperial documents went to her for the seal that made them law. Finally, she was the mother of most of his children. During the course of their nineteen-year marriage, they had fourteen children, though only seven lived into adulthood.

Khurram's father placed him at the head of the imperial armies, and he scored great victories for the empire. In 1617 his grateful

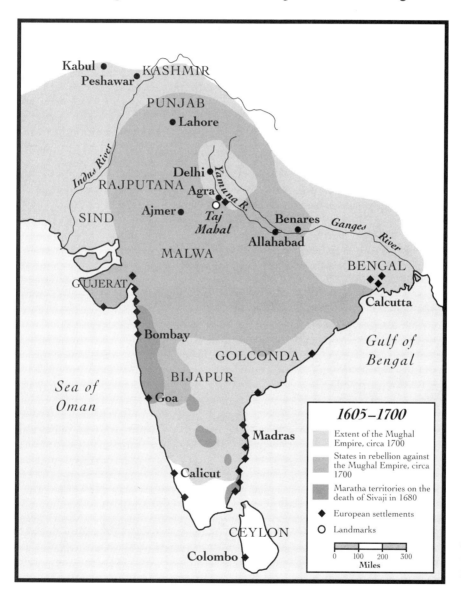

THE MUGHAL EMPIRE AT THE HEIGHT OF ITS TERRITORIAL EXPANSION

father awarded him the exalted title Shah Jahan. Gifts of priceless jewels, robes of honor, ceremonial swords, rare horses, and valuable elephants poured in from his father and Nur Jahan. At this point he was clearly the heir to the throne and exercised tremendous power as part of the quartet that ran the empire.

When Shah Jahan finally won the throne in 1627, it was after almost five years of rebellion against his father. Now that he was in control, he immediately took steps to clear away any possible rivals. He ordered the murder of certain relatives, including his brother Shariyar, a nephew, and some cousins. This was the first time in Mughal history that a brother shed his own family's blood.

Shah Jahan finally ascended the throne to the great acclaim of the people of Agra. He settled into Akbar's vast Red Fort palace with his wife and children, secure for the first time after years on the run. The harsh times were behind him as he took control of the empire.

The Taj Mahal

Alas! This transitory world is unstable, and the rose of its com-
    fort is embedded in a field of thorns.
In this world, there is an ancient tradition:
Sweet pleasure is not without bitterness.

—from the *Padshah Nama* by Muhammad Amina Qazwini

In 1631 the pregnant queen accompanied her husband and the court to the city of Burhanpur, in the south. Shah Jahan had gone there to conduct military campaigns in the region of the Deccan. While there, in the midst of giving birth to their fourteenth child, Mumtaz Mahal died.

Shah Jahan was senseless with grief. He wailed that his life had lost all meaning and shut himself off from everyone for a week. He put on white robes, the dress of mourners, and offered heartfelt prayers for his wife's departed soul. He wept so often that his eyes

TAJ MAHAL COMPLEX, GENERAL VIEW. *Photograph courtesy the American Institute of Indian Studies, Varanasi.* This view shows the gardens leading up to the central mausoleum with the mosque on the left and the guest house on the right. The Yamuna River flows just behind the mausoleum.

were weakened and he had to wear spectacles from then on. His grief physically transformed him, for his beard turned gray from shock and sadness.

Shah Jahan renounced all pleasure for two years after his wife's death. He gave up fine clothing and his beloved gems, music, singing, and the rich banquets that were so much a part of his imperial life. His daughter Jahanara, then seventeen, had been with her mother when she died. She took over Mumtaz Mahal's official duties, and also assumed responsibilities for raising the imperial family. She consoled her father in his bottomless grief.

Mumtaz Mahal's body was temporarily laid to rest in a garden pavilion at Burhanpur, but six months later it was conveyed all the way to Agra. Along the way, at each stopping place, prayers were offered, and food and money distributed among the needy. The emperor had purchased a large site in Agra for her mausoleum. It was on the river, close enough to the palace that it could be easily viewed. The site lay among the beautiful garden palaces of the aristocracy, which lined the river. There her body was again temporarily laid to rest while her magnificent tomb was commenced.

The Illumined Tomb

And he shall reward their constancy with a Garden, and silk:
And when thou lookest, there shalt thou behold Bliss and a realm
    magnificent

The poetry of the Quran beautifully depicts the Gardens of Paradise that await the departed faithful. To the Mughals gardens were an earthly reflection of heaven itself. Those who were prominent or saintly enough to merit an elaborate tomb always had it placed in a garden. For the Mughal emperors, a tomb was an opportunity to honor the dead, heed their religious duty, and broadcast their magnificence. For Shah Jahan it was all of this and more. He set out to build a heavenly palace to house his beloved empress's remains.

When Shah Jahan commenced building his wife's tomb, in 1632, he had already shown a great interest in architecture and planning. His powerful grandfather also loved to build, but Shah Jahan surpassed even him. His reign became universally renowned for its magnificent architectural achievements. The most famous, by far, was the tomb that he built for his wife, the Taj Mahal.

The Imperial Tomb

In planning the empress's resting place different requirements had to be fulfilled. It had to be a tomb complex set within beautiful gardens. But it was also a religious site. There was a mosque and a ceremonial guest house. Its immense outer courtyard contained arcades with housing, inns, and even shops. These provided services for the many people who visited the tomb, among them pilgrims.

Some of them came to seek blessings from the departed empress's spirit. According to the tradition of the *Hadith,* the commentaries on the sacred Quran, a woman who died in childbirth attained the status of a blessed martyr. Within the tomb itself, prayers and recitations from the sacred Quran were perpetually offered. Even today this practice continues. One can hear the haunting sounds of this chanting as it rises up and echoes within the lofty dome.

Finally, the empress's tomb was the setting for the annual feast that was held on the anniversary of her death. The ceremony always began at night. The gardens were illuminated with torches while rich carpets and tents covered the grounds. The guests included the imperial family, courtiers, scholars, clerics, and reciters of the Quran. Religious texts and special poetry were chanted and Shah Jahan himself recited the *Fatiha*, the opening verses of the Quran. Incense was burned, fragrant scents offered, and a lavish meal prepared. At the end generous amounts of money were distributed to the clerics and the poor. The following day the ceremony was repeated again for the women.

Planning the Tomb

To this day scholars do not know who actually designed the Taj Mahal. Many theories have been advanced over time, even attempts by Europeans to credit this masterwork to one of their own countrymen at Shah Jahan's court. Today, some scholars suggest that the tomb's designer might have been Ustad Ahmad Lahori, an architect in the court of Shah Jahan. Their evidence includes some verses from a poem written by his son, Lutf Allah Muhandis, himself a court architect to Dara Shikoh, the emperor's son. His poem includes the following lines of praise for his father:

> At the orders of the world-conquering king,
> He constructed the edifice of the tomb of Mumtaz Mahal

Whether his claim is actually true is still not known.

In the Mughal era, there were no special schools or licenses for

TAJ MAHAL MAUSOLEUM,
VIEW OF EASTERN ARCHWAY.
*Photograph courtesy the American
Institute of Indian Studies,
Varanasi.*
Floral decorations are set into
the white marble walls over
this magnificent archway.
Above that, and running on
both sides of the arch are
graceful calligraphic inscriptions set into the marble as
well. Many of these are quotes
from the Quran or special
poetry. The court calligrapher,
Amanat Khan, designed all of
the calligraphy, and highly
skilled artisans cut the stones
and laid them into the carved
channels in the marble.

architects. They were considered master masons, like the builders of
Europe's gothic cathedrals. The title *Ustad* signified master, and
when it was used with the word *mi'mar*, or mason, it meant "master
builder." In Ustad Ahmad Lahori's case, he was not only a builder
and engineer, but a scholar of astronomy, geometry, and mathematics. Building was his family's profession, and his sons followed in his
footsteps.

The Work Commences

The emperor engaged two supervisors to oversee the project. They were 'Abd ud-Karim and Makramat Khan, the minister of public works, one of the most important nobles of the realm. Workers were brought in from around the empire and as far away as Persia and Central Asia. There were stonecutters, carvers, inlayers, and fine carvers. These last artisans created jewel-like decorations similar to those of the nearby I'timad ud-Daula Tomb. The eminent calligrapher and courtier Amanat Khan was engaged to design the religious and poetic inscriptions that graced the surface of the buildings.

The riverside site was prepared by constructing a deep foundation set on arches. This engineering provided for possible flooding during the annual monsoon season. An ingenious waterworks was devised to provide water within the tomb and for the garden's fountains. Water was lifted from the river, raised in several stages, and stored in three overhead tanks. From there pipes conveyed the water into the building, and a separate system led into the garden. It is said that thousands of people worked on the building. Construction began in 1632, and by 1643 the tomb, its gardens, and most of its buildings were finished.

The Taj Mahal Today

The tomb itself is entirely sheathed in white marble inlaid with delicate calligraphy and floral decorations. Its central dome rises higher than a twenty-three-story building, and at each corner of the massive platform, four ornamental marble minarets rise one hundred and thirty-two feet in height.

Because the tomb is a holy site, shoes must be removed before climbing the stairs of its white marble platform. The stairs lead up to the building itself, where a carved garden of delicate blooms graces its lower walls. Once inside, an eight-sided chamber rises to the lofty dome. All is hushed and cool within its beautiful walls, and the light, no matter how harsh outside, falls gently within. It filters in, softened by tiny mosaics of milky white glass set in delicate marble window screens. The silence inside is sometimes broken by the chanting of Muslim prayers. These lush Arabic chants rise up and fill the dome and then descend to bless the memory of Mumtaz Mahal and Shah Jahan, who lies buried next to her. Their exquisite stone monuments lie side by side beneath the dome. Surrounding them is a pierced marble screen whose intricate, lacy walls are set with semiprecious stones.

The actual tombs lie in a chamber below. At first they were covered by sheets of pearls, but these were stolen more than one hundred years later, when the empire was in shambles. Massive silver doors of extraordinary workmanship once guarded the domed tomb's entrance. They too were carried off by marauding soldiers and melted down. At one time the interior was hung with chandeliers and covered in precious carpets, but all that has long since gone.

What does remain is the spectacular *pietra dura* work that covers the interior and exterior of the tomb structure. Precious and semiprecious stones were brought from many lands to create intricate images of flowers and decorative designs. There is jade from China, turquoise from Tibet, lapis lazuli from Afghanistan, amethysts from Persia, agates from Yemen, mother-of-pearl from the Indian Ocean, and diamonds from the Golconda mines in the Deccan. The work is so fine that you can find tiny flowers with more than fifty separate stones in them. There are literally hundreds of these blossoms covering the screens, cenotaphs, and parts of the walls.

For all of their beauty, these ornaments are not what make the Taj Mahal great. Instead, it is the harmony which unites the whole building. The Taj Mahal surpassed anything ever attempted before, and that harmony was Shah Jahan's greatest accomplishment.

Shah Jahan's gardens looked different from those of today. They were filled with the Mughals' favorite blossoms—tulips, crocuses, and dahlias—and heavily planted with all types of trees. The grounds were far more shady, colorful, and fragrant then. They were also more peaceful. Now they have been planted with sweeping lawns and accommodate masses of tourists who flock there to visit one of the acknowledged wonders of the world.

Shah Jahan's choice of marble, from nearby Rajasthan, was one of his most inspired decisions for the building. Apart from its design, the Taj Mahal's most magical quality is the way it changes its appearance in the shifting light of the day. The early morning tints it a light, delicate blue, while the midday bleaches it white as a bone. By late afternoon it begins to glow golden, and it assumes rosy hues in the setting sun. It turns most regal in the full moon of October, the Sharad Purnima, when it glows like an immense pearl.

Today Mumtaz Mahal's exquisite monument lies next to Shah Jahan's, bathed in the gentle light that falls beneath the Taj Mahal's dome. The inlaid calligraphy that graces its side are verses from the Quran, and they were chosen by her husband.

> Truly the righteous shall be in Bliss,
> Upon raised couches, gazing.
> Thou shalt observe in their faces the radiancy of Bliss!

He had made the very image of paradise for his beloved wife, and for his own magnificent memory as well.

Shahjahanabad

Shah Jahan's great love of splendor was also revealed in the city he built at Delhi, Shahjahanabad. It was started in 1639 and took ten years to complete. When it was done it was one of Asia's, if not the world's, greatest cities. A long straight street called the Chandni Chowk ran through the capital from the gates of the palace. At its

THE TAJ MAHAL

The delicate tracery work on the interior of the dome. *Photograph courtesy the American Institute of Indian Studies, Varanasi.*

Inside the Taj Mahal's domed main chamber. The lacy marble screen, inlaid with semiprecious stones, surrounds Shah Jahan's and Mumtaz Mahal's monuments. *Photograph courtesy the American Institute of Indian Studies, Varanasi.*

A detail from the outside walls, carved gardens of white marble. *Photograph courtesy the American Institute of Indian Studies, Varanasi.*

THE TAJ MAHAL'S NAME

Shah Jahan did not name his wife's resting place the Taj Mahal. He referred to it as the Rauza-i Munavvara, the "Illumined Tomb." The name Taj Mahal is thought to be a contraction of the empress's name, Mumtaz Mahal. The English traveler Peter Mundy, writing about his journey to Shah Jahan's empire, referred to the departed empress by the name "Tage Maholl," and other Europeans did the same. It would seem that the tomb was commonly called by her name shortly after it was built.

center flowed a beautiful tree-lined canal, while broad terraces and arcades lined its length. Nobles built fine palaces and mosques within the new city, and in a very short time it became a great metropolis.

The core of Shahjahanabad was its palace complex, virtually a city within a city. The palace was designed as a vast rectangle set within massive walls. One long side of the rectangle ran along the Yamuna River, while the other faced the city. Within the palace everything was designed on an irregular grid. The city side was the more public side of the complex while the river side was reserved for the emperor and the harem.

The private area of the palace was filled with lush gardens surrounding airy marble pavilions topped with golden cupolas. Streams ran in sculpted marble channels through the palaces themselves and out to the gardens. The delicate sounds of flowing water continuously echoed through these beautiful halls. It was in these exquisite chambers that Shah Jahan began his day.

The Emperor's Day

Shah Jahan's daily life shuttled back and forth between the private and public spaces of his palace. He awoke well before dawn in his private section of the palace, the Khas Mahal. He spent his nights in the Khwabagah, or sleeping chamber, an arched white marble riverside pavilion. After performing his morning bathing rituals, he repaired to a small nearby prayer room for the first of his five daily prayers.

The emperor's first public obligation was his daily sunrise appearance to his subjects gathered on the riverbank below. He would enter the bastion known as the Mussaman Burj and go to the window known as the *Jharoka-i Darshan*. There he would simply appear in the window as the sun came up. The Mughal emperors followed this custom as a way of assuring the populace that they were alive and in control.

Just before eight o'clock Shah Jahan had his first audience, or *durbar*, held in the impressive Diwan-i 'Am, the Hall of Public Audience. Each day the emperor appeared before the assembled nobles and public here. It was a spacious, many-pillared pavilion that fronted on a huge courtyard where the public assembled. The hall was hung with beautiful brocade awnings and spread with rich silk carpets. Golden and silver railings enclosed the sections for the nobles, and the emperor gave audience while seated in his elevated marble throne.

DIWAN-I 'AM, HALL OF PUBLIC AUDIENCE, *Red Fort, Delhi, 1639–49, old postcard.* This photograph, taken in the early part of this century, shows the grand Hall of Public Audience at Delhi's Red Fort. Since Shah Jahan's time, the fort was plundered by the Persians and partially destroyed by the British, but this hall survived and its beautiful architecture gives a hint of its former splendor.

This was a highly ceremonial occasion, with the massed trumpets and drums of the palace orchestra playing a fanfare from their hall above the courtyard. The emperor mounted his elevated throne from behind. On either side of him stood his sons, the imperial princes. Just beyond them his attendants and standard bearers stood at attention, golden banners and ceremonial fly whisks in hand.

In front of the emperor stood his nobles, ranked within their special spaces. At this time reports and petitions were presented by the military, courtiers, and provincial officials. Appointments and honors were announced as well. Religious affairs were dealt with and

SHAH JAHAN IN *DURBAR*, *ca. 1630, by Bichitr, from the* Padshahnama. *The Royal Collection, Her Majesty Queen Elizabeth II.* With jewel-like precision, Shah Jahan's masterful court painter Bichitr captured a moment in the daily audience ceremony of *durbar.* Here, on an elevated throne, Shah Jahan embraces one of his sons, who bows in homage. His other sons and his chief minister, Asaf Khan (Nur Jahan's brother), stand nearby. Below and before him are his highest nobles, while just beyond the railing stand the lesser nobles.

charitable donations granted. Finally there was a magnificent procession of horses and elephants from the imperial stables. In all, the ceremonial audience usually lasted for two hours.

After that Shah Jahan moved to the Hall of Private Audience, the splendid Diwan-i Khas. This was where he met with his Council of Ministers. The real policy decisions of the empire were discussed and debated here. It was also the hall where the emperor greeted foreign ambassadors, who must have been awed by its opulence.

The ceiling was covered with beaten silver and the walls, like the Taj Mahal's, were inlaid with semiprecious stones. In this hall stood the fabled Peacock Throne, ablaze with the glitter of priceless jewels. Shah Jahan had commissioned this masterpiece to display his amazing collection of gems. The throne was designed as a raised platform whose canopy was supported by twelve elegant pillars, and it took his workmen seven years to create.

The Frenchman Jean-Baptiste Tavernier actually saw this legendary throne. He was one of the foreign jewel merchants who had come to Hindustan to sell the emperors gems. He reported that the twelve columns were each studded from top to bottom by rows of large, perfect pearls. The canopy itself was crowned by a golden peacock whose tail sported a fortune in sapphires. On either side golden floral bouquets glittered with blossoms of precious gems. Fringes of pearls hung from the top of the canopy while diamonds shimmered above the emperor's head.

Leaving the Hall of Private Audience, Shah Jahan had one more meeting, this time with the imperial princes and a few selected ministers. When this was over, it was usually past noon and time for lunch. He took his lunch in the harem, where, like all people in Hindustan, he ate sitting on the floor. Fine cloths were spread to protect the rich carpets and upon them gold and silver dishes were placed. He was served by two beautiful women who knelt by his sides. An endless variety of delicacies was presented, but despite this abundance it is said that Shah Jahan's favorite dish was the surprisingly common rice and lentil preparation called *kichri.*

When he had finished with his lunch, the emperor took a brief rest in the harem. Then he held court especially for the members of the harem and dealt with all of its business for the day. There would be petitions from the ladies and grants of monies administered to special women's charities or individual cases that the noble ladies had heard about.

Following that it was time for the midday prayers at three o'clock. On Fridays he would be conveyed in a solemn procession to the nearby cathedral mosque, the Jami Masjid. There, within the immense expanse of its courtyard, surrounded by his court, he bowed in prayer toward Mecca. He had built this house of worship, the largest mosque in all of Hindustan. With its three majestic domes, towering minarets, and turreted gateways, it was the last great architectural work of his reign.

Shah Jahan grew up to be a considerably more conservative Muslim than his predecessors. Early in his reign, he began to reverse their religious policies, ordering the destruction of certain Hindu temples and prohibiting the construction of new ones. As he grew older, though, his policy began to soften, influenced by his more liberal older children.

On normal weekdays he would attend prayers in one of the halls of the palace and then retire to his private apartments. Often there was more administrative work that required his presence back in the Diwan-i Khas. Sometimes there would be a chance to watch the elephant fights held below his quarters on the riverbank, or to watch dancers perform in the harem. By eight o'clock he would return to the harem for dinner and be entertained by female musicians. Shah Jahan was particularly fond of music and supported some outstanding Hindu musicians.

He went to bed at around ten o'clock and, like his grandfather, had readers who read stories to him. One of his favorite books was the *Baburnama,* which he would listen to as he drifted off to sleep. He was fond of his adventurous ancestor and loved hearing the stories of his life.

The business of being emperor took place within a setting of great opulence, but it was business nevertheless. At least he had his children to help him. Since his wife's death, he had increasingly relied on his children to assist him with the empire. One of them, Aurangzeb, was a brilliant military leader who was often dispatched to fight for his father. Shah Jahan's favorite, however, was kept home by his side. His name was Dara Shikoh.

The Tragic War

Shah Jahan's four sons were Dara Shikoh, Shah Shuja, Aurangzeb, and Murad Baksh. The two most significant players in the looming tragedy were Dara Shikoh and Aurangzeb. They were polar opposites in many ways. Even more important, they represented two different paths for Mughal history. Dara Shikoh followed the route of Akbar, whose spiritual heir he was. His impulse was toward interreligious cooperation and tolerance. Aurangzeb, on the other hand, yearned for the purity of a Muslim state that followed the hallowed traditions of the Quran. His route was toward restoring the state religious orthodoxy that Akbar had tried to weaken.

Dara Shikoh was Shah Jahan's eldest and most beloved son. The emperor let all know that the prince was his intended heir and kept him close to home in hopes that he would not rebel. Shah Jahan did not want his son to follow in his father's footsteps. While Dara Shikoh stayed on in the imperial court, he cultivated the spiritual and scholarly side of his personality. He was also an accomplished patron of the arts.

The prince had a deeply mystical streak and was attracted to the Muslim philosophy of the Sufis. Although Sufi beliefs varied widely at that time, Dara was inclined to the more Hindu influenced branches of Sufi thought. Like Akbar, he kept company with Hindu sages, and as time went on his involvement with Hindu thought deepened. He even translated the Hindu Upanishads into Persian.

Shah Jahan and his firstborn son, Dara Shikoh, were especially close. In this formal riding portrait by Govardhan, Dara Shikoh respectfully follows his father and shields him with a royal parasol, an Indian symbol of kingship.

Dara Shikoh's translation eventually became the one known to the West and was read in English translation by such distinguished American thinkers as Ralph Waldo Emerson.

Dara Shikoh lived in far more conservative times than had Akbar. The state religious establishment, the ulama, had grown stronger through the years, encouraged by his own father. It cast a suspicious eye on the prince's religious interests and activities.

Despite his spiritual interests, Dara Shikoh was hardly a saint. He was keenly aware that his brothers were all potential rivals for the throne. Although his father wanted him to be the next emperor, he knew that he would have to defeat his brothers if the throne were really to be his. He used his influence with his father to weaken his brothers' interests at court, and even their careers. His great rival was his ambitious younger brother Aurangzeb.

While Dara was mystical and scholarly, Aurangzeb was a hard-headed military man. He was highly learned, spoke many languages, and started out as an outstanding patron of the arts, but his chief talents were military and administrative. His brilliance as a general won many victories for his father. Aurangzeb was also a deeply conservative Muslim who supported the religious establishment. He viewed his brother's religious experimentation with a distaste bordering on condemnation. Yet, since Dara was clearly in favor, Aurangzeb could say or do little to stop his older brother.

While both princes were ambitious Aurangzeb possessed a single-minded determination that surpassed his brother's. He was deeply suspicious by nature and not above using deceit to gain his ends. Aurangzeb had suffered greatly as a result of Dara's scheming. Despite his military achievements, he had been practically demoted in rank and had fallen from favor with his father. He would even the score later on, but in the meantime he used his masterful talents for manipulation to help gain the throne.

AURANGZEB, ca. 1700, artist unknown. Courtesy the Board of Trustees, Victoria and Albert Museum, London. Aurangzeb's profile was distinctive, with his erect bearing and long straight nose. The last great Mughal emperor was a military man at heart, and he toughened his body by eating simply, fasting regularly, and sleeping on the ground covered only with a tiger skin. This formal portrait gives a sense of his strong will and determination.

The Beginning of the End

His opportunity came in September of 1657. Shah Jahan had fallen seriously ill, and all of his sons assumed that he was about to die. They feverishly prepared to go to battle for the throne and, although their father finally recovered, a full-blown war broke out, which lasted for two years. In the midst of the war, in 1658, Aurangzeb had himself crowned emperor and took the title *Alamgir*, "seizer of the world." In the end he prevailed and went on to kill and imprison his other brothers and their children. By eliminating all of his rivals, he

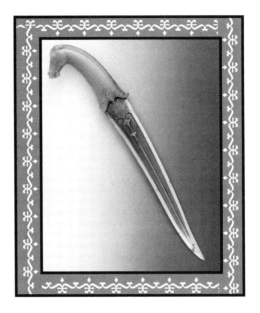

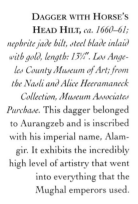

DAGGER WITH HORSE'S HEAD HILT, *ca. 1660–61; nephrite jade hilt, steel blade inlaid with gold, length: 13¾". Los Angeles County Museum of Art; from the Nasli and Alice Heeramaneck Collection, Museum Associates Purchase.* This dagger belonged to Aurangzeb and is inscribed with his imperial name, Alamgir. It exhibits the incredibly high level of artistry that went into everything that the Mughal emperors used.

assumed full command of the imperial armies, who now pledged loyalty to him alone. His rival, Dara Shikoh, was captured and brought to Delhi. Aurangzeb arranged for him and his young son to be paraded before Delhi's populace in disgrace.

The French doctor François Bernier witnessed this gruesome parade. The princes were seated backward on a worn-out, filthy elephant. They were wrapped in rags covered with dirt while a slave sat behind them brandishing a drawn sword. Bernier recounted:

> The crowd assembled upon this disgraceful occasion was immense; and everywhere I observed the people weeping, and lamenting the fate of Dara in the most touching language. . . . From every quarter I heard piercing and distressing shrieks, for the Indian people have a very tender heart; men, women, and children wailing as if some mighty calamity had happened to themselves.

Shortly afterward, Dara Shikoh was tried for religious heresy and executed.

Just before his sons were destroyed, Shah Jahan was imprisoned by Aurangzeb in the Agra Fort. The aging emperor had given total control of his forces to Dara Shikoh. When he defeated Dara, Aurangzeb tried to lure his father from the impregnable Red Fort. Shah Jahan refused to budge and only surrendered after a short, effective siege. Aurangzeb knew that the emperor's sympathies lay completely with his enemy, Dara Shikoh, and kept him under close watch. Finally he decided to pay his father a formal state visit, but just as his procession neared the fort's entrance, he was shown a secret letter that had been intercepted from Shah Jahan. It was intended for Dara Shikoh and promised him full support. Aurangzeb turned around and canceled the visit. He never saw his father again.

With Aurangzeb in full control of the military, Shah Jahan was imprisoned for the remaining eight years of his life at Agra. It was much too dangerous for Aurangzeb to have the embittered former emperor set free. The other alternative, his father's murder, would be one of the greatest sins a Muslim could commit. There were rumors afloat at the time that Aurangzeb tried to have his father poisoned, but it is not known whether they were true. The easiest option for Aurangzeb was to keep his father under perpetual house arrest until he died.

Shah Jahan's daughter, Jahanara, was imprisoned along with him and his harem. She comforted him for his remaining years, one small consolation for the destruction of his family by his least favorite son. He exchanged many harsh letters with Aurangzeb over the years, until the new emperor finally deprived him of pen and paper to write. He had already lost many of the privileges of his earlier life. There were no elephant fights to watch anymore, no courtly business to transact, and no solemn processions to visit his wife's tomb on the anniversaries of her death.

Toward the end of his life, Shah Jahan's rancor toward his son seemed to soften. He became more devout and studied the sacred Quran frequently. He said his prayers while fingering his exquisite prayer beads comprised of perfect pearls. A few years before,

Aurangzeb had demanded them, but the old man wrote angrily to his son that he would sooner smash them into powder than part with them.

Shah Jahan might have stood on the terrace and watched the setting sun paint the Taj Mahal in hues of pink and gold. He had built all of this: the swelling domes before him and the luxuriant pavilions behind. He could have thought back to another place that he had built, a place that he would never see again: his palace at Delhi, now Aurangzeb's home. There, within the splendid hall that housed his Peacock Throne, he had inscribed a poem on the arch overhead. An expression of happiness, of absolute delight in all that he had made, it said:

> If there is a Paradise on the face of the earth,
> It is this,   it is this,   it is this

Epilogue: The Final Days

Shah Jahan died on January 22, 1666, and was buried next to his wife in the Taj Mahal. Aurangzeb ruled for forty-nine years, until his death in 1707, as long a reign as his great-grandfather Akbar. Of all the great Mughal emperors, Aurangzeb remains the most controversial. To many Muslims he is a hero, a leader who attempted to restore the cherished values of their religion to the empire. They admire his simple piety and point out that while he had great power he also humbly copied out Qurans and knitted skull caps as acts of faith. Even today people come to pay their respects at his tomb, and one of New Delhi's most beautiful streets is named in his honor.

Most Hindus feel that he was an oppressor who sought to return their people to second-class status. The debate is as active today as ever, and close inspection reveals that Aurangzeb's record was not nearly as black or as white as his supporters and detractors would have us believe. While Akbar's longevity strengthened and secured the empire, Aurangzeb's ultimately did not. In some ways the seeds of the empire's destruction were already there, but Aurangzeb's actions hastened its downfall. The major problem, and one that Aurangzeb would tenaciously pursue until his dying day, was the Deccan.

The Deccan was the challenge that loomed increasingly larger, from Akbar's final days on. With its huge army, the Mughal Empire had to keep expanding, but by Aurangzeb's time there were few places left to conquer. Probing northward toward their ancestral lands was no longer a possibility. Shah Jahan had sent forces to conquer Transoxiana, but they had failed. Not only that, but Qandahar, the key northern fortress, had fallen to the Persians, leaving the northwest border vulnerable. There was nowhere left to go but south, deeper into the subcontinent, and the Deccan soon ensnared Aurangzeb's forces in its tangles.

The Deccan's independent Muslim kingdoms were largely Shiite Muslim, while Aurangzeb was fervently Sunni. The Deccan kingdoms were constantly fighting and making alliances among themselves and even with the Mughals when it served their interests. They also gave aid to the Mughals' enemies, the Hindu Marathas, based in the west-central part of the subcontinent. The Marathas' great military leader, Shivaji, developed his forces into a formidable power during Aurangzeb's reign. Their guerrilla tactics, used in the Deccan's hilly western lands, proved a serious challenge to the Mughal emperor's forces.

Aurangzeb determined to expand into the Deccan kingdoms and wipe out the growing Maratha threat as well. In 1681 he turned his forces south and left his capital at Delhi. For the next twenty-six years, he stayed in the south and personally directed his military campaigns, never to return north again. Slowly and methodically he set about bringing order to the region through an endless series of military campaigns that lasted until his death. All of his military genius was directed toward this goal, and finally the massive Mughal forces managed to subdue the Deccan.

Under Aurangzeb, all of the Deccan kingdoms, including wealthy Golconda with its diamond mines, were taken over, and the Mughal Empire grew to its greatest size. Yet the Deccan conquests were not conclusive, due to the uncontrollable Marathas. Their guerrilla warfare and deep grassroots Hindu support ensured that Aurangzeb's forces were always harassed. This was a war fought under different terms than Akbar's great conquests. There were fewer nobles here like the Rajputs who were willing to join the empire. There was no way to fully consolidate Mughal victories in the hilly lands and shifting borders of the Deccan. Controlling the region was a huge drain on the empire's resources.

Other serious problems lay just beneath the surface. Once Aurangzeb left Delhi, the capital of the empire became the huge, mobile military city that surrounded the emperor. The business of governing the rest of the empire began to falter as Aurangzeb's obsession with the Deccan dominated all other concerns. At the same time, his conservative Muslim religious policies alienated many of the Rajputs and other powerful Hindu groups.

Aurangzeb was a superb leader whose grip on the empire remained firm even in his last years. Despite that, just before he died in 1707, he had become deeply disillusioned over the state of the empire. Pious as ever, he also worried about his fate in the world to come. In a revealing letter to one of his sons he wrote: "I came alone and go as a stranger. I do not know who I am, nor what I have been doing. I have sinned terribly and do not know what punishment awaits me." In keeping with his orthodox Muslim beliefs and spartan lifestyle, Aurangzeb decided that his tomb would be utterly simple, unlike those of his predecessors. He lies buried in an unpretentious grave in Khuldabad, a village of the Deccan. The region that was his obsession became his gravesite as well.

Aurangzeb lived so long that his son Mu'azzam was quite old when he ascended the throne as Bahadur Shah. Like Aurangzeb's other children, he had spent much of his time in prison, placed there by his father. Even the emperor's daughter, Zeb un-Nisa, a talented poet, was imprisoned for the last twenty-one years of her life. None of his heirs had any practical experience of rule. Typically, when Aurangzeb died, yet another bloody war of succession broke out. By its end five princes were dead.

From that point on the empire slowly slid downward. The Deccan quickly broke free of Mughal control, with some areas falling to the Marathas and others becoming part of the new Muslim kingdom of Hyderabad. The growing power of the Punjab-based Sikhs, a religious group formed in Mughal times, began to threaten Mughal interests in the north. Then the Jats, a warlike tribe in the center of the empire, began to raid Mughal settlements. Finally the Rajputs, already alienated, broke free of Mughal control. Emperor followed emperor in quick succession, and even safe territories held back money from the rulers. As territory and power declined, so did Mughal wealth.

In 1739 the empire experienced its first death blow. Nadir Shah, the Persian ruler, invaded a weakened Hindustan, conquering Delhi. In one day his forces massacred many of its inhabitants, and later they carried off the dynasty's remaining wealth, including the Peacock Throne. The carefully crafted throne was taken back to Persia, where it was broken up for its jewels. Around this time the Taj Mahal was plundered as well.

While all of this was happening, a new power was rapidly growing on the Indian subcontinent, that of the colonial British. Starting from their early days in Jahangir's reign as traders for the East India Company, the British had established ports and trading posts on India's coasts. Their settlements in Bombay, Calcutta, and Madras thrived and grew to become large cities. By the eighteenth century, the British had begun to battle against the French for control of India's coasts. They soon proved the victors. Slowly but steadily they became involved with the local rulers, winning concessions and gaining land and control. By the early nineteenth century, British power on the subcontinent had grown so strong that the weakened Mughal emperors were taken under their protection. For the next fifty-four years they became virtual puppets, until the Sepoy Revolt in 1857, a failed rebellion against British rule.

The last Mughal emperor, the aged Bahadur Shah II, was exiled to Burma in 1858 for his role as reluctant figurehead of the rebellion. His sons did not survive him. During the fighting, they hid at Humayun's tomb, but surrendered to the victorious British when the revolt failed. They were shot in cold blood by the British major who captured them. The Mughal Empire was no more.

A new empire, the British Raj, rose to fill the vacant shoes of the Mughals. In 1858 the ruling East India Company was dissolved and India became a crown colony headed by a viceroy, who ruled in the name of the English monarch. In 1877 the English queen, Victoria, was crowned empress of India. The new empire was a mixed blessing for India's peoples. The country saw tremendous economic development. Many railroads, roads, harbors, new cities, and extensive irrigation projects were built. A new Indian middle class and civil service was created, which had access to European education. On the other hand, the British government discriminated in favor of products made in England, such as textiles. Indian producers could not compete. Laws and economics began to destroy the ancient economy of the villages. Poverty and unemployment grew dramatically.

The British learned from the Mughals. They kept local rulers in power if they were pleased with their performance, but let go others who fell from their favor. The kingdoms of rulers who died without heirs became the property of the colonial government. But England's manipulation of the relationship between India's Hindus and Muslims was in its own self-interest, not based on Akbar's enlightened rule. The British desperately needed to maintain control and subtly but effectively pursued a policy of dividing the two religious communities. The more they fostered conflicts between the Hindus and Muslims, the weaker their combined threat to British rule. With the foundation of the Indian National Congress in 1885, the subcontinent's leaders began to assert their own power. Although the British

Viceroys House New Delhi

THE VICEROY'S HOUSE,
NEW DELHI, *old postcard.*
The architects for New Delhi
were Sir Edwin Lutyens and
Sir Herbert Baker. The cen-
terpiece for their new city was
the viceroy's palace, depicted
here shortly after it was completed in 1929. Today it is
called the Rashtrapati Bhavan
and is the official residence of
the president of India.

began to make some concessions to their Indian subjects, demands
for greater control of their own land grew.

In the midst of this, in 1911, the British decided to move their capital from Calcutta, on the east coast, to Delhi, the former Mughal
imperial capital. Not since Shah Jahan had constructed his great
city had anyone built a new capital at Delhi. Now, with intentions
every bit as imperial as Shah Jahan's, they created New Delhi, a
great planned city. At its heart rose the viceroy's palace, a massive
domed building larger than the palace of Versailles in France.
Behind the palace, the British created beautiful Mughal-style gardens, which remain to this day.

This imperial city was officially inaugurated in 1931, but just sixteen years later the British gave it up to the newly independent government of India. In that year, 1947, two sovereign states were
created from the former crown colony: India and Pakistan. Pakistan
was made up of the two primarily Muslim areas: the western Punjab
and Sind, and the eastern portion of Bengal. There were many,
including the great Gandhi, who were against the religious partition

of the subcontinent, and now their worst fears were realized. No sooner was independence granted than a vast and tragic exchange of populations took place between the two new countries. As Hindus left Pakistan for India and Muslims departed India for Pakistan, violent conflicts broke out and many thousands were slaughtered. Communities that had been living side by side for centuries were shattered overnight.

Today India, like other nations with diverse religious communities, continues to struggle with these conflicts. Most pressing is the relationship between the Hindus and the Muslim minority, but there are issues with the Sikh minority as well. These were concerns that the Mughals also dealt with, but in a different context. Their main concern as a Muslim minority was finding a way to rule effectively over a Hindu majority. Akbar found practical solutions that honored his subjects' beliefs and benefited the empire. Following in his footsteps, the government of India's founders took special care to ensure that their nation's constitution protected all religious minorities. India's challenge now is to maintain this noble ideal.

The Mughal heritage is still very present in northern India. Tourists flock to visit the emperors' masterworks like Fatehpur Sikri, the Red Fort, and the Taj Mahal. They eat Mughlai cuisine in restaurants and buy souvenirs based on Mughal artistic traditions. Mughal history is still debated by scholars and historians. Were they foreign oppressors who built their splendor on the backs of the Hindu masses, or enlightened rulers who gave the country a measure of stability and relative prosperity? Was Akbar really as tolerant as his legend maintains, and were Aurangzeb's religious policies truly as discriminatory? There is much more to learn about the dynasty, and deeper exploration is needed. Despite the imperial memoirs, court histories, and travelers' accounts, many mysteries remain. Mughal history is much like its paintings, filled with crystal clear details placed in elusive settings.

India has seen many rulers rise and fall. Since ancient times, many invaders have swept over the land only to disappear into history's shadows. Not the Mughals. In the world's memory, their legacy gleams as brightly as one of Shah Jahan's fabulous gems. They were warriors, as hungry for power and land as any group in history, and yet they were more. They arrived in India with a history and ideal of civilized life. On its soil they set about creating that life, and in the process invented new forms of art and beauty. They learned from the land they had won and, in time, became part of it.

The greatest Mughal emperors left the world a valuable heritage. Akbar showed that peace could exist between different faiths only if it was promoted from above. And Shah Jahan showed that perfection could exist in an imperfect world. He created it. The Taj Mahal was his vision of Paradise on earth, conceived for remembrance, and built from love.

TAJ MAHAL FRAMED BY AN ARCH, *photograph by Luis Villela. Government of India Tourist Office, New York.*

Timeline

1368	Ming Dynasty established in China and rules until 1644
1405	Death of Amir Timur, Babur's ancestor and founder of the Timurid Empire
1483	Babur born in Ferghana, Transoxiana, in Central Asia
1492	Seeking a westward sea route to India, Christopher Columbus sails to the Americas, which were later called the "West Indies"
1498	The Portuguese navigator Vasco da Gama finds the sea route to India around the Cape of Good Hope, South Africa
1504	Babur conquers Kabul
1505	Beginning of Portuguese commercial empire in South and East Asia and the establishment of the port of Goa, on India's western central coast in 1510
1506	The construction of Saint Peter's Basilica commences in Rome, with the participation of Michelangelo, Bramante, and Raphael
1519	The Portuguese navigator Ferdinand Magellan, in the service of Spain, undertakes the first voyage to circumnavigate the globe

1519	The Spanish conquistador Hernán Cortés begins his conquest of the Aztec Empire of Mexico
1520	Suleiman the Magnificent becomes head of the Ottoman Empire
1526	Battle of Panipat; Babur takes control of the sultanate of Delhi
1527	Battle of Khanua, Babur's victory over the Rajput confederacy
1530	Death of Babur; his son, Humayun, succeeds him
1539	Humayun defeated by the Afghan Sher Khan at the Battle of Chausa, and in 1540 at the Battle of Kanauj
1540	Beginning of Sur dynasty of Sher Shah, formerly Sher Khan, which lasted until 1545
1547	Ivan IV (the Terrible), crowned tsar of Russia, expands the empire south and takes over the Muslim khanates of Kazan and Astrakhan
1556	Death of Humayun; son Akbar, age thirteen, becomes king under the regent Bairam Khan
	Akbar wins the second Battle of Panipat against Hindu forces led by Hemu
1558	Elizabeth I ascends the English throne
1562	Akbar marries the daughter of the Hindu Raja of Amber, she is named Maryam az-Zamani
1564	Abolishment of the *jizya* tax on non-Muslims
1568	Akbar conquers Chittorgarh
1569	Birth of Akbar's son Salim at the hermitage of Shaykh Salim ud-Din Chishti
1571	Work starts on Fatehpur Sikri
	The Battle of Lepanto takes place, in which Ottoman naval dominance in the Mediterranean is broken by combined Catholic forces led by Spain

1572	In France, the St. Bartholomew's Day Massacre occurs—20,000 Protestants are murdered by Catholic forces for both religious and political reasons
1575	The Ibadatkhana, the House of Worship, created at Fatehpur Sikri
1577	Birth of Mihr un-Nisa at Qandahar
1580	First Roman Catholic priests arrive in Fatehpur Sikri from Goa
1588	Destruction of the Spanish Armada by the English under Elizabeth I
1589	Henri IV ascends the throne in France, unites the nation, and promotes tolerance for Protestants in the Edict of Nantes (1598)
1592	Birth of Prince Khurram, son of Prince Salim
1600	British East India Company is founded; within two hundred fifty years it would spread its rule over much of India
1601	Prince Salim begins his half-hearted rebellion against Akbar
1603	Establishment of the Tokugawa shogunate in Japan with its capital at Edo (Tokyo); the shogunate would rule until 1867
1605	Death of Akbar; Prince Salim ascends throne as Jahangir
1607	English settlers arrive in Jamestown, Virginia
1611	Jahangir weds Mihr un-Nisa (Nur Jahan)
1612	Khurram weds Arjumand Banu (Mumtaz Mahal)
1616	The English ambassador Sir Thomas Roe arrives at Jahangir's court
1618	Birth of Aurangzeb, son of Prince Khurram and Arjumand Banu

1619	Jahangir builds the Shalimar Gardens in Kashmir
1620	Puritan separatists make voyage from England on the *Mayflower* to establish a colony in Plymouth, New England
1622–28	Nur Jahan builds her parents' tomb known as the tomb of I'timad ud-Daula in Agra
	Rebellion of Shah Jahan against Jahangir
1627	Death of Jahangir; Shah Jahan becomes emperor
1631	Death of the Empress Mumtaz Mahal
1632	Shah Jahan begins construction of Mumtaz Mahal's tomb, the Taj Mahal
1639	Shah Jahan's new capital, Shahjahanabad, started at Delhi
1640	Prince Dara Shikoh, Shah Jahan's eldest son, translates the Hindu Upanishads into Persian
	British East India Company establishes a trading port at Madras, on the southeast coast of India
1643	Louis XIV ascends the throne in France
1646	Shah Jahan begins campaign to reclaim the Mughal homeland, Transoxiana
1657	Shah Jahan falls critically ill and his sons scramble to claim the throne
1658	Aurangzeb wins the war for succession to the Mughal throne and is crowned Emperor Alam-gir
1666	Death of Shah Jahan, after eight years' imprisonment in the Agra Red Fort palace
1669	Uprising of the Jats, Hindu peasants in central Hindustan
1680	Death of the Hindu Maratha leader Shivaji

1681	Alamgir moves south to the Deccan to deal with conflicts there
1696	Peter I (the Great) becomes sole ruler of Russia
1707	Death of Alamgir
1739	Delhi invaded and plundered by the Persian Nadir Shah; the Peacock Throne is carried off to Persia
1776	American colonies declare their independence from England
1857	The Sepoy Revolt, an Indian rebellion against British rule, breaks out, but is put down
1858	The last Mughal emperor, Bahadur Shah II, is exiled by the British for his role in the rebellion. The Mughal Empire is formally ended
1877	Queen Victoria of England is crowned empress of India
1947	The British partition their colony of India, creating two new states, India and Pakistan

Glossary

Abbreviations: S = Sanskrit   H = Hindi   P = Persian   A = Arabic   T = Turkish

Many of the words in this glossary are Persian, Arabic, or Turkish. In the case of Arabic and Turkish words I have given the Persian pronunciation, which would have been used by the Mughals. In Persian the following letters have these corresponding English sounds:

aa	like	_author_	ch		_church_
a		b_ad_	kh		the "ch" in the Scottish
eh		b_e_d			word "loch"
ee		r_ee_d	zh		the "j" in the French word
o		_jello_			"je"
oo		b_oo_k			
ow		n_ow_			

AGRA   H. (_aagra_) A city in northern India that was one of the three capitals of the Mughal Empire; site of the Taj Mahal and the Red Fort

AKBAR   P. (_akbar_) (b. 1542–d. 1605) The greatest of the Mughal emperors, who established the empire

AKBARNAMA   P. (_akber-naameh_) The _Book of Akbar_, a three-volume history of Akbar's life and reign, compiled by Abu'l Fazl up until his own death in 1602; it was illustrated by the painters of Akbar's court studios

ALAMGIR   P. (_aalamgeer_) "seizer of the universe"; title adopted by Aurangzeb when he ascended the throne in 1658

AMIR   T. (_ameer_) "Lord"; title used by the military nobility of Central Asia

AMIR TIMUR   T. (_ameer taymoor_) (b. 1336–d. 1405) Descendant of Jenghiz Khan and ancestor of Babur who established the Timurid Empire in Central Asia centered in his capital at Samarqand

ARYANS   P. (*aareeyans*) Northern warrior peoples who invaded India in approximately 1500 B.C., bringing new language, religion, and customs with them

ARYAVARTA   S. (*aareeyavrrtah*) The heartland of the culture of the Aryan peoples in India, the Ganges plain

ATMAN   S. (*aatmen*) The Hindu term for soul

AURANGZEB   P. (*aawrangzayb*) (b. 1618–d. 1707) Son of Shah Jahan and Mumtaz Mahal; last great emperor of the Mughal dynasty

BABUR   T. (*baahboor*) (b. 1483–d. 1530) Founder of the Mughal dynasty, born in Ferghana, Transoxiana

BEG   T. (*beg*) A title, originally Turkish, meaning "Lord"

BEGUM   T. (*begoom*) A title, originally Turkish, meaning "Lady"

BHARAT   S. (*bharet*) Ancient Sanskrit term for the land of India, derived from the mythological king Bharata

BIRYANI   P. (*beryanee*) A preparation of rice with meat or vegetables that is one of the main dishes of Mughlai cuisine

BRAHMA   S. (*braamah*) The Hindu creator god, part of the Hindu divine trinity of Brahma, Shiva, and Vishnu

BRAHMIN   S. (*braamen*) The highest of the four Hindu varnas, traditionally the priests

CALIPH   A. (*kaylif*) Muslim ruler's title; traditionally the leader of the Sunni Muslim world after the death of Prophet Muhammad

CHAJJA   H. (*chajjah*) Thin sloping projection of stone resembling a cornice

CHARBAGH   P. (*chahar baagh*) Four-square Persian-style garden

CHATTRI   H. (*chetree*) Umbrella-shaped dome or pavilion

CHAWPAR   H. (*chowpar*) A game similar to Parcheesi

DARSHAN   S. (*dahrshun*) "Viewing"; in the Hindu religion, viewing the image of the god as an act of worship and receiving an auspicious glance in return

DARWAZA   H. (*durvaza*) Gate, as in the gate to a city or fortress

DECCAN   H. (*daykhan*) "The south"; to the Mughals, the part of India below the Vindhya mountain chain

DELHI   H. (*daylee*) Northern Indian city that was one of the three Mughal imperial capitals, now the capital of India

DEVI   S. (*dayvee*) The mother goddess of the Hindu religion, worshiped in many forms

DHARMA   S. (*darma*) The cosmic order of the universe in the Hindu religion

DIN-I ILAHI   A. (*deen-ee-eelahee*) A semireligious brotherhood, founded by the Emperor Akbar in 1582

DURBAR   H. (*durbar*) Ceremonial royal audience

FATEHPUR SIKRI   H. (*fataypoor seekree*) Palace city near Agra founded by Emperor Akbar in 1571

FATIHA   A. (*faatiheh*) The opening lines of the Holy Quran, which have special significance in the Muslim religion

FERDAUS MAKANI   P. (*ferdos makanee*) "Placed in heaven"; the honorary name given to Emperor Babur after he died

FIRMAN   P. (*farman*) Imperial decree

GANGA   S. (*gaangah*) The Hindu river goddess who dwells in the Ganges River; also the Hindi name for the river

GHAZI   A. (*gaazee*) "Warrior of Islam"; honorary title given to those who fought for the Muslim faith

GURKANI   T. (*goorkaanee*) The Mughal name for their dynasty, derived from one of the titles of their ancestor Amir Timur

HADJ   A. (*hadge*) The pilgrimage to Mecca; one of the Five Pillars of Islam

HARIJAN   H. (*hareejahn*) "Children of God"; name given by the twentieth-century Indian leader Mohandas K. Gandhi to the people outside of the varna system, traditionally the lowest in status

HEGIRA   A. (*hijra*) The flight of Prophet Muhammad from Mecca to Medina on June 15, 622, the date on which the Islamic calendar begins

HINDUSTAN   P. (*hindoostaan*) Traditional Persian and European name for India

HUMAYUN   P. (*homayoon*) (b. 1508–d. 1556) Mughal emperor, son of Babur and father of Akbar

IBADATKHANA   P. (*ehbadat khaneh*) "House of Worship"; hall constructed by Emperor Akbar at Fatehpur Sikri in 1575 for religious discussions and debates

ISLAM A. (*eeslaam*) "Submission"; the name of the Muslim religion, which stresses submission to the will of God

JAGIR H. (*jagir*) Nonhereditary land given by the Mughal emperors to their nobles as payment for services

JAHANGIR P. (*jahangeer*) (b. 1569–d. 1627) "World Seizer"; Mughal emperor, son of Akbar and father of Shah Jahan

JAIN H. (*jane*) A follower of Jainism, one of India's oldest religions; Jainism does not glorify an absolute god, but rather focuses on self-perfection as a means to attain liberation

JALI H. (*jolly*) Pierced ornamental stone screen

JATI H. (*jatee*) Known as "caste" in English; the thousands of subdivisions of varnas in the Hindu social system

JAUHAR H. (*johar*) Form of ritual suicide by burning practiced by the wives of Rajput warriors when defeat was imminent

JHAROKA-I DARSHAN H. (*jerokah*) Balcony; palace window from which the Mughal emperors appeared to their subjects every morning at sunrise

JIHAD A. (*jehad*) Islamic term for "Holy War," like the Crusades

JIZYA A. (*jezyeh*) An annual tax imposed on nonbelievers by Muslim law

KARKHANA P. (*karkhaneh*) Imperial workshops in the palace, producing everything from fine weavings and perfumes to arms and cookware

KARMA S. (*karmah*) The Hindu doctrine of cause and effect

KHAN T. (*khaan*) A Mongol/Turkic term for "Lord," used by the military nobility

KHAN-I KHANAN P. (*khaanee khaanan*) "Lord of Lords"; title given to the supreme military commander of the Mughal imperial forces

KHURRAM P. (*khoorram*) Birth name of Shah Jahan (b. 1592–d. 1658)

KHUTBA A. (*khotbeh*) Proclamation and blessing announcing the rule of a king, read to the congregation in the mosques on Friday

KITABKHANA P. (*kitabkhaneh*) The "House of Books"; the imperial workshop for book production, painting, and translating; also the imperial library

KULFI H. (*koolfee*) The Mughal form of ice cream, still made to this day in India

LAHORE H. (*lahoar*) One of the three Mughal imperial capitals, now in Pakistan

MADRASA   A. (*maadraseh*) College for Muslim studies; first developed as an institution independent of the mosque in Central Asia

MAHABHARATA   S. (*mahabarat*) *The Great Epic of the Bharata Dynasty;* one of the two great Hindu epics and the longest poem in the world, it depicts a cataclysmic war between two dynasties

MAHAL   H. (*muhull*) Palace

MAHARANA   H. (*maharahnah*) "Great King"; title given to the Hindu Rajput rulers of Mewar

MAYDAN   P. (*meydan*) Playing field and open area for gatherings used in Mughal and Persian cities

MIHRAB   A. (*mehraab*) A central niche in the wall of the mosque that faces in the direction of Mecca

MI'MAR   P. (*mehmaar*) A mason, builder, or architect

MINAR   A. (*mehnaar*) A tower

MINARET   A. (*mehnaaret*) The tower of a mosque from which the muezzin proclaims the call to prayer five times daily

MIRZA   T. (*mehrzaa*) "Prince"

MONGOL   (*mahngoal*) An English word, derived from the Persian Mughal, describing a nomadic, warlike people of the Central Asian steppes who swept a conquering path across much of Asia and Eastern Europe beginning in the early 1200s; their leader, Jenghiz Khan was an ancestor of Babur

MONSOON   H. (*mahnsoon*) The annual rains that fall on the Indian subcontinent; the summer monsoon falls from June to early September, while the winter monsoon falls in December and January

MOSQUE   A. (*maask*) Muslim house of worship

MUEZZIN   A. (*moazzen*) In the Muslim religion the man who chants the call to prayer five times daily at the mosque, usually from the minaret

MUGHAL   P. (*mooghaal*) "Mongol"; the name for the dynasty founded by Babur; this name was given first by the Persians and later by the Europeans, but it was not a name that they gave their own dynasty; they called themselves the Gurkani dynasty; Europeans called the emperors the "Great Mughals"

MUGHLAI   P. (*moogleh*) The name for the imperial cuisine of the Mughals, a rich and subtle cooking still practiced in northern India

MUMTAZ MAHAL (P. *momtaaz* H. *muhull*) the "Chosen of the Palace"; Shah Jahan's empress, who died in 1631; her mausoleum is the Taj Mahal

NADIR AZ-ZAMAN P. (*naaderazzaman*) the "Wonder of the Age"; title given to the Mughal court painter, Abu'l Hasan, by his patron, Emperor Jahangir

NAUROZ P. (*nowrooz*) Persian New Year's festival that falls in the early spring; it was first celebrated at the Mughal court by Emperor Akbar and was one of the great annual court festivals until the time of Emperor Alamgir (Aurangzeb), who discontinued its celebration

NAZIR P. (*naazer*) "Guardian"; title given to eunuchs in their capacity of guarding the ladies of the imperial harem

NILGAI H. (*neelguy*) An animal native to India that is related to the antelope, also called the "blue bull" for its color

NUR A. (*noor*) "Light"

NUR JAHAN A., P. (*noor jahaan*) (b. 1577–d. 1645) "Light of the World"; Jahangir's wife and empress, and the most prominent woman in Mughal history

PADSHAH P. (*paadshaah*) An independent ruler without an overlord; Babur took this title and from then on all Mughal emperors were known as Padshah

PADSHAHNAMA P. (*paadshaahnaameh*) The chronicles of the first two decades of Shah Jahan's reign (1627–47), written by Abdul Hamid Lahori and illustrated by court painters

PALKI H. (*palkee*) A litter in which Mughal nobles would travel; it was usually carried by four men, and sometimes more, depending on how elaborate it was

PARSI H. (*parsee*) The Parsees (plural of Parsi) follow the ancient Zoroastrian religion of Persia, which they brought to India when they fled Muslim persecution beginning in A.D. 766; there are fewer than 100,000 Parsees in the entire world, and many of them live in the Indian port of Bombay

PISHKASH P. (*peeshkesh*) Gifts for the Mughal emperors that the nobles would offer on special occasions; the emperor would choose which of the nobles' gifts he preferred and return the rest of them

PUNJAB H. (*poonjaab*) The largely flat, prosperous farming region that now straddles northern India and Pakistan; Lahore, now in Pakistan, was the traditional capital of the Punjab and one of the three Mughal imperial capitals

PURDAH A. (*pardeh*) The seclusion of women, traditionally practiced by Muslims and wealthy Northern Hindus

QAMARGAH P. (*ghamargaah*) "Place Shaped Like the Moon"; the name for a type of hunting in which animals were driven into a large enclosure and then hunted within it

QIBLA A. (*ghebleh*) Direction for Muslim prayer

QURAN A. (*ghoraan*) The sacred book of the Muslims, which they consider the word of God as given to Prophet Muhammad

RAJPUT H. (*raajpoot*) In Mughal times the Hindu warrior clans and their leaders who lived in the hills and deserts of northwestern India

RANA H. (*raanaa*) "King"

RAUZA P. (*rowzeh*) A large Muslim tomb, often set in a garden

SALAT A. (*salaat*) Prayer five times a day, the second of the Five Pillars of Islam

SAMARQAND T. (*saamaarkaand*) A city in Central Asia, in the region of Transoxiana; former capital of the empire of Amir Timur and one of the most important cities of Babur's time; now it is located in the Republic of Uzbekistan

SANSKRIT (*sanskreet*) The ancient literary language of Hindu Indian culture

SART P. (*saart*) Persian peoples of Central Asia

SERAI P. (*saraay*) Also called "caravanserai," a resting place for merchants and travelers

SHAHADAH A. (*shahaad*) The Muslim confession of faith: "There Is No God But Allah, and Muhammad Is His Prophet"

SHAH JAHAN P. (*shaa jahaan*) (b. 1592–d. 1666) Mughal emperor, son of Jahangir and father of Dara Shikoh and Aurangzeb; builder of the Taj Mahal

SHAMYANA H. (*shamyana*) An awning, usually colorfully decorated

SHAYKH P. (*shaaykh*) A Sufi religious leader

SHIA A. (*sheeeh*) Also called the Shian-i-Ali, or partisans of Ali; this Muslim sect believes in the legitimate spiritual religious leadership of the imam, not the caliphs; they are the chief minority sect in the Muslim world and predominate in Iran

SUFI T. (*soofee*) The Sufis are the chief mystical sect of Islam and have played an important role in the Muslim world of India

SUNNI A. (*sonnee*) The Sunni are the majority Muslim sect in the world; they believe in the legitimate spiritual descent through the caliphs

TARAH P. (*tarh*) A plan used by builders

TASLIM   P. (*tasleem*) A reverential salute, usually to the emperor; the person saluting touches his forehead with his right hand and then performs a full bow and prostration

TILAK   H. (*teelaak*) Among the Hindus, a colored mark placed on the forehead as a sign of religious devotion

TRANSOXIANA   (*traansoxeeana*) The region of Central Asia between the Oxus and Jaxartes rivers; in the time of Amir Timur and Babur it was home to a number of important cities, including Samarqand

ULAMA   A. (*olahmaa*) The state Muslim religious establishment—the clergy, scholars, and religious judges hired by the imperial administration

UPANISHADS   S. (*upaneeshads*) A collection of Hindu religious texts that were composed between 700 and 500 B.C.; this deeply philosophical work is central to the Hindu religion

UZBEKS   T. (*oozbehks*) A northern Central Asian Turkic-Mongolian people who eventually conquered the territories of the former Timurid Empire in the time of Babur

VARNA   S. (*verna*) "Color"; the four divisions of Hindu society dating from Aryan times; the four varnas were: brahmins, or priests; kshatriyas, the kings and warriors; vaishyas, the merchants and farmers; and shudras, the laborers

ZAKAT   A. (*zakaat*) The giving of alms to the poor, one of the Five Pillars of Islam

ZENANA   P. (*zanaaneh*) The imperial harem

Further Reading

There are few books written specifically for young-adult readers on the Mughal dynasty. However, one that includes information about the Mughals is:

Exploration into India by Anita Ganderi. New York: New Discovery Books and Macmillan, 1994. This book has many illustrations and deals with India both during and after the coming of the Europeans.

There are many scholarly books for adults about the Mughal dynasty, but among the best books for a general audience are:

The Great Mughals by Bamber Gascoigne, with photographs by Christina Gascoigne. London: Jonathan Cape Ltd., 1971. The Gascoignes' work sets the standard for books about the Mughals. It is solidly researched and told in a way that brings the dynasty to life. There are many illustrations, including on-site photographs.

The Romance of the Taj Mahal by Pratapaditya Pal et al. Los Angeles: Los Angeles County Museum of Art; London: Thames and Hudson, 1989. This catalog, published in connection with a major exhibition at the Los Angeles County Museum of Art, tells the story of Shah Jahan's reign and the Taj Mahal. It contains much useful information and many beautiful illustrations.

India: Art and Culture 1300–1900 by Stuart Cary Welch. New York: Holt, Rinehart, and Winston and Metropolitan Museum of Art, 1985. This catalog, published in connection with a major exhibition at the Metropolitan Museum of Art, explores the world of Indian art and culture from early times until the end of the last century. It is a great book to look at, with page after page of color reproductions, including old photographs. There is an extensive section on the Mughals.

Delhi, Jaipur, Agra: India's Golden Triangle. APA Publications Ltd., 1991. This guidebook, part of the Insight City Guide series, has wonderful color photographs of these three Indian cities. There are many images of Mughal buildings, and there is a good text. Even if you are not planning a visit to India, this will give you a feel for the country and a glimpse at some of its treasures.

Delhi and Agra: A Traveller's Companion by Michael Alexander. New York: Atheneum, 1987. This is part of a worldwide series that matches historical travelers' descriptions with actual sites in the world. You can read Amir Timur's description of his conquest of Delhi; Babur's lamenting over the lack of gardens in Agra; and François Bernier's chronicle of a day at Shah Jahan's glittering court at Delhi. This book, along with a good picture book (like the guide listed above), can help bring Mughal history alive.

Cultural Atlas of India by Gordon Johnson. New York: Andromeda Oxford Ltd. and Facts on File, 1996. This is part of a series that covers world cultures. It is well written and contains many photographs and illustrations of artwork. There is a large section on the Mughals and their heritage.

Quotes in the text are taken from:

Baburnama: Memoirs of Babur, Prince and Emperor. Translated and edited by Wheeler M. Thackston, Jr. Oxford University Press, New York, 1996

Delhi and Agra: A Traveller's Companion by Michael Alexander. Atheneum, New York, 1987

The History of India, As Told by Its Own Historians by Sir Henry Miers Elliot and Prof. John Dowson. Originally published in 1867, reprinted by Low Price Publications, Delhi, India, 1996

Sources

There are a number of sources that provided background historical information for this project. They include: *A New History of India,* by Stanley Wolpert, Oxford University Press, 1977, *The History & Culture of the Indian People, The Mughal Empire,* edited by R. C. Majumdar, Bharatita Vidya Bhavan, 1974, *Muslim Civilization in India,* by S. M. Ikram, Columbia University Press, 1964, *The History of India, As Told by Its Own Historians* by Sir H. M. Elliot and John Dowson, Low Price Publications, 1996, *Cultural Atlas of India,* by Gordon Johnson, Andromeda Oxford Limited, 1996, and *The Great Moghuls* by Bamber & Christina Gascoigne, Jonathan Cape, London, 1971.

Art and architectural information on India and the Mughals was provided by: *The History of Architecture in India,* by Christopher Tadgell, Phaidon Press Limited, 1990, *Mughal Architecture,* by Ebba Koch, Prestel Verlag, 1991, *Architecture of Mughal India,* by Catherine B. Asher, Cambridge University Press, 1992, *Mughal India, Architectural Guides for Travellers,* by G. H. R. Tillotson, Penguin Books, 1991, *Indian Miniatures of the Mughal Court,* by Amina Okada, Harry N. Abrams, 1992, *India, Art and Culture 1300–1900,* by Stuart Cary Welch, Holt, Rinehart and Winston, 1985, *Arts of India 1550–1900,* edited by John Guy and Deborah Swallow, Victoria and Albert Museum, 1990, and *The Penguin Guide to the Monuments of India, Vol. II,* by Phillip Davies, Penguin Books, 1989.

CHAPTER ONE

Sources for this chapter include *Travels in the Mughal Empire* (Low Price Publications, 1994), the memoirs of the French doctor François Bernier, who spent six years (1658–1664) in the Mughal Empire. Bernier left descriptions of the Imperial Palace built by Shah Jahan at Delhi, and of Mughal court ceremonies. Bernier personally witnessed some of the dramatic events surrounding Shah Jahan's sons' struggle for the throne. Like many Europeans reporting on their time in the Mughal Empire, his sources were largely secondhand, including bazaar gossip and reports from certain informants at court.

Information on Islam came from a variety of sources, including *Muhammadan Festivals* by G. E. Von Grunebaum, Olive Branch Press, 1988. Some of the Mughal examples explaining the Five Pillars of Islam come from *The History of India, As Told by Its Own Historians* by Sir H. M. Elliot and John Dowson, Low Price Publications, 1996. This eight-volume series is based on translations of original sources collected by Sir H. M. Elliot (b. 1808–d. 1853) and John Dowson (b. 1820–d. 1881). I used sections from this work for source material throughout this book.

CHAPTER TWO

All quotations from Babur's memoirs, the *Baburnama*, were from the version translated and edited by Wheeler M. Thackston, Oxford University Press, 1996.

Information on the land of India and the Hindu religion came from a variety of sources, including *Hindu Art,* by T. Richard Blurton, British Museum Press, 1992, *The Wonder That Was India,* by A. L. Basham, Grove Press, Inc., 1959, *Hindu Goddesses,* by David Kinsley, University of California Press, 1988, *Cultural Atlas of India,* by Gordon Johnson, Andromeda Oxford Limited, 1996.

CHAPTER THREE

Much of the material for this chapter, and all quotes by Babur, come from Wheeler M. Thackston's new edition and translation of the *Baburnama*, mentioned above. The book's introductory essays give background information about the culture that Babur grew up in. Another source was *The Great Moghuls,* by Bamber Gascoigne, Jonathan Cape, London, 1971.

Information on Mughal gardens came from *The Garden,* by Julia S. Berrall, Penguin Books, 1966, and *The Gardens of Mughul India,* by Silvia Crowe, Thames and Hudson, 1972.

CHAPTER FOUR

Sources for this chapter included the Wheeler M. Thackston edition of the *Baburnama*, from which sections of Babur's letter to Humayun are quoted. The quotes from Khondamir are taken from his *Humayun-nama,* in the fifth volume of *The History of India, As Told by Its Own Historians,* by Sir H. M. Elliot and John Dowson. Also from that volume are quotes from the *Tazkiratu-l Wa'kia't* of Jauhar, Humayun's faithful valet. Bamber Gascoigne's *The Great Moghuls* provided a great deal of information on Humayun's life.

Information on Mughal painting came from *Imperial Mughal Painting,* by Stuart Cary Welch, George Braziller, 1978, and *The Imperial Image,* by Milo Cleveland Beach, Freer Gallery of Art, 1981.

CHAPTERS FIVE AND SIX

There are many sources for these two chapters about the Emperor Akbar. They include sections of Volumes Five and Six from Elliot and Dowson's *The History of India, As Told by Its Own Historians,* including extracts from the *Akbarnama,* by Abu'l Fazl, and the *Muntakab al-Tawarikh* by Abd ud-Karim Kadir Badaun.

Two books by Michael Brand and Glenn D. Lowry, *Akbar's India,* Asia Society Galleries, NY, 1985, and *Fatehpur Sikri: A Sourcebook,* the Aga Khan Program for Islamic Architecture at MIT & Harvard, 1985, gave detailed information about the artistic heritage and daily life of Akbar's court. An issue of the Indian Arts Magazine *Marg,* Volume XXXVIII, No. 2, devoted to Fatehpur Sikri, contained many interesting articles as well. Finally, there were some helpful essays and beautiful photos to study in the Insight City Guide, *Delhi, Jaipur, Agra,* APA Publications (HK) Ltd., 1991.

CHAPTER SEVEN

Sources for this chapter, and all quotes from Jahangir, are from his memoirs, the *Tuzuk-i-Jahangiri,* translated by Alexander Rogers and edited by Henry Beveridge, Atlantic Publishers and Distributors, 1989.

Information on Nur Jahan and life in the imperial harem came from a number of sources, the chief one being *Nur Jahan,* by Ellison Banks Findly, Oxford University Press, 1993. Another source which was useful for impressions of the princely life of the Mughal and Rajput courts was *A Second Paradise, Indian Courtly Life 1590–1947,* by Naveen Patnaik, Doubleday & Co, Inc., 1985.

CHAPTER EIGHT

There were three major sources for this chapter. The first was *Romance of the Taj Mahal,* Los Angeles County Museum of Art, Thames and Hudson, 1989. This beautifully illustrated catalog describes the world of Shah Jahan and the masterpiece that he commissioned, the Taj Mahal. The second source was a catalog from the Metropolitan Museum of Art, *The Emperor's Album,* Harry N. Abrams, 1987, which presents portions of a painting album commissioned by Jahangir and Shah Jahan. The final source was *Taj Mahal, The Illumined Tomb,* by W. E. Begley and Z. A. Desai, University of Washington Press, 1989. This is an anthology about the Taj Mahal that presents seventeenth-century Mughal and European sources. It includes translations of all of the verses inscribed on the tomb.

Index

Page numbers in *italics* refer to illustrations and captions. Terms with asterisks (*) appear in the Glossary.